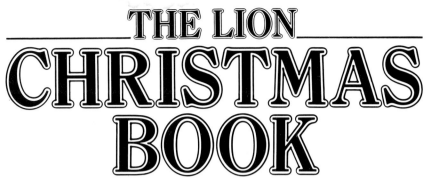

THE LION
CHRISTMAS
BOOK

WRITTEN AND COMPILED BY MARY BATCHELOR

A LION BOOK

Copyright © 1984 Lion Publishing

Published by
Lion Publishing plc
Icknield Way, Tring, Herts, England
ISBN 0 85648 535 7 (casebound)
ISBN 0 7459 1220 6 (paperback)
Albatross Books Pty Ltd
PO Box 320, Sutherland, NSW 2232, Australia
ISBN 0 86760 482 4 (casebound)
ISBN 0 86760 852 8 (paperback)

First edition 1984
Reprinted 1985
This paperback edition 1986

British Library Cataloguing in Publication Data
Batchelor, Mary
     The Lion Christmas book.
     1. Christmas—Juvenile literature
     I. Title
     394.2′ 68282 GT4985
     ISBN 0 7459 1220 6

Illustrations
Ann Blockley, pages 28, 30-31, 54-55, 78-79;
Ray Burrows, pages 22-23; Vicky Emptage,
pages 11, 58; Jane Fort, pages 14, 34, 46;
Martin Salisbury, pages 16-17, 18-19;
Gillian Hurry, pages 38-39, 44-45, 82;
Caroline McDonald-Paul, pages 8, 12, 36-37,
76; D'reen Neeves, pages 70-71, 72;
Charles Penny, pages 24-25; Carol Tarrant,
pages 56-57

Photographs
Paul Craven, page 44;
James Davis Worldwide Photographic Travel
Library, page 40, carol singers in Victorian
costume, Christmas Steps, Bristol, England;
Keith Ellis ARPS, pages 35, 59; Mary Evans
Picture Library, page 29, Christmas at
Windsor, 1848; Sonia Halliday Photographs,
page 88, the presentation of Jesus at the
Temple, nineteenth-century stained glass
window at Chesham, Bucks, England; Frank Lane
Agency/C. West, page 81, hoar frost on spider's
web; Lion Publishing/David Alexander, page
13, Bethlehem bells; MEPhA/Alistair Duncan,
pages 50-51, shepherds on the hills of
Bethlehem; Tiophoto/Ulf Siöstedt, pages 26,
Swedish girl on St Lucy's Day; Vision
International/Anthea Sieveking, page 91,
/M. Seraillier, page 82; Mike Elkner,
page 43, celebration in Australia;
ZEFA, endpaper picture, pages 9, 11 advent crown,
14, St Nicholas and Black Peter, 27, 29, 47, 53,
68, New Guinea village, 76, the star-singers

Cover photo: ZEFA

Printed and bound in Italy

CONTENTS

TIME TO CELEBRATE

Christmas is the time for —
presents,
food,
church,
parties,
holidays
— and all sorts of other good things. That's because Christmas is a time for celebration. It's the birthday of Jesus.

When a new baby is born, there is great excitement in the family. Everyone wants to tell the news. At Christmas we talk about the good news of the birth of Jesus. We sing carols, send cards, perhaps make little crib scenes, or act the story of the first Christmas.

And we celebrate Jesus' birth by going to church, where we can join with other people in singing his praises and thanking and worshipping him, just like the shepherds and wise men so long ago.

We also celebrate Jesus' birthday by having parties with exciting food, just as we do when anyone in the family has a birthday. There are presents to choose and wrap — gifts to be received and opened too.

This book is all about celebrating Christmas — in many ways — in different countries of the world. We remember again what happened at the first Christmas and we think of things to do and enjoy, as we have all the fun and excitement of keeping Jesus' birthday almost two thousand years later.

CHOOSING A BIRTHDAY

Everyone has a birthday. The 25th of December was chosen for Jesus' birthday because no one knew the actual day or date of his birth. We can, of course, be absolutely certain that he *was* born. Luke, in his New Testament Gospel, tells us it happened when the Roman Emperor Augustus ruled the world. But he doesn't give us the day or the month. That may be because people then did not bother as much about birthdays as we do now.

The eastern part of the church decided to celebrate Jesus' baptism, and later his birth, on January 6. Christians in Russia and other countries still keep Christmas on that day. And in Armenia January 19 is Christmas Day. But in many parts of the world December 25 is kept as Jesus' birthday.

It all goes back to the days of the Roman Empire — because the Romans already celebrated the festival of Saturnalia in December. The general holiday gave Christians time for their own celebrations. Then, when St. Augustine came to England to preach the gospel about two hundred years later, Pope Gregory advised him to keep the dates of the pagan feasts but give them new meaning by using them for Christian festivals. So the old Scandinavian mid-winter Yuletide festival was transformed into the birthday feast of Jesus Christ.

It may seem a strange coincidence that so many countries in Europe had holidays and festivals in December. But it is not really surprising. For, in this part of the world, December comes at the darkest and deadest time of the year. So people have always needed some kind of celebration to cheer themselves up. In the old, pagan days they also hoped to bring back the light and life of springtime by performing special ceremonies.

The joyful celebration of Jesus' birth when everything is at its darkest reminds us all that God's own light has come into our world, lifting darkness and conquering evil for ever.

Many of the Christmas customs we enjoy today are left over from long ago, from the days before December was taken over as Jesus' festival. Giving presents, eating special foods, decorating homes, lighting candles, all began in the long distant past. Because these customs were so deeply rooted in the minds and memories of the people, the Christian leaders often had to let them stay. But they were given new meanings. For example, the holly, once a pagan symbol of luck and new life, became instead — with its prickles and red berries — a picture of Christ's crown of thorns and of his blood given for us.

Our Christmas customs may be mixed with old superstitions and forgotten beliefs, but with Jesus' coming they have been given new life. Jesus is at the heart of Christmas.

THE VERY IMPORTANT GUEST

66 *Dear God,*
Christmas should be earlier because kids can only be
good for so long. **99**
Beth
From CHILDREN'S LETTERS TO GOD

W hen someone you like is coming to stay, you may find it hard to wait for the day to arrive. But there are all kinds of things to do first, in order to be ready for the visitor.

The Christian church calls the four weeks before Christmas 'Advent' and that word means 'coming'. It is the time of year when we get ready for the coming of the most important Guest of all time — Jesus Christ.

Advent reminds us of three different 'comings' of Jesus. The first is in the past. It happened long ago at the first Christmas. Jesus, God's Son, who made our world, came to live in it as a baby, then as a boy, and a man who gave his life to bring us close to God. The second 'coming' belongs in the present because Jesus is waiting to come now to every person who invites him into his heart and life. The third

'coming' of Jesus is still in the future. One day Jesus will come back to our world, not as a little, helpless baby, but as King and Judge of all.

So Advent is the season for getting ready — ready to understand the true meaning of Christmas, ready to ask Jesus into our lives and ready for the day when he will come again.

66 *At Advent we should try the key to our heart's door.*
It may have gathered rust. If so, this is the time to oil
it, in order that the heart's door may open more easily
when the Lord Jesus wants to enter at **99**
Christmas time!
A NEW GUINEA CHRISTIAN

AN ADVENT CALENDAR TO MAKE

You can buy Advent calendars in the shops but it is more fun to make your own. They usually show a house with windows, each hidden by a flap of paper, with pictures underneath. You can begin using the calendar on 1 December and as each day comes you open a window, marked by a number, to discover the picture beneath. Instead of a house for background you could use a large Christmas tree.

1
First draw and colour your house or tree on a large piece of card. It may help to use a ruler and to draw lightly in pencil first.

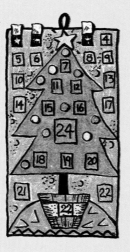

2
Mark out 23 small window spaces and one large one for 24 December.

3
Now draw pictures to stick over the empty window squares — or cut them out of old Christmas cards. Here are some suggestions for the pictures: the angel Gabriel, Mary, Joseph, the star, the town of Bethlehem, wise men, shepherds, the angel choir, sheep, donkey, camels, a manger. Don't forget that the last picture, for 24 December, should show the whole manger scene.

4
When you have glued each picture into place, cut out small pieces of paper to act as shutters to cover the pictures. Glue them in place at the top only. Number each window on the outside of the shutter.

5
Fix a piece of ribbon to the back with sticky tape and you can hang up your calendar for all the family to enjoy.

ADVENT 'CROWN'

An Advent 'crown' is a circle of four candles which stands on the table or may be hung from the ceiling by ribbons. It is sometimes made of straw or evergreen twigs, but here is a simple version that you can easily make yourself.
You will need:
two potatoes
four candles
aluminium foil
sprays of greenery

1
Cut the two potatoes in half and scoop out a hole in each piece at the centre of the rounded side. An apple corer will make a neat hole that will safely hold the candles.

2
Cover the potato halves in foil and stand firmly on a plate or aluminium foil dish.

3
Arrange sprays of holly and ivy or laurel around them, pushing the stems into the potato, so that they remain fresh. You can also use sweet-scented rosemary spikes, a great favourite for Christmas decoration long ago.

4
Now put your four candles into the potatoes and your crown is ready to use.

5
Light the first candle on the first Sunday in Advent, two candles on the second Sunday, three on the third — until all are alight on the Sunday before Christmas. The candles remind us that when Jesus came he brought the light of God's love and truth into our dark world.

TELL THE GOOD NEWS!

Angels, from the realms of glory,
Wing your flight o'er all the earth;
You who sang creation's story
Now proclaim Messiah's birth:
Come and worship Christ the new-born King.
FRENCH CAROL

Nowadays not many people see angels, although they are still busy in our world, serving God and taking care of his children. When it was time for Jesus to be born, God chose angels to bring the good news to earth.

First of all, Gabriel, a very important angel, was sent to tell Zechariah that his wife Elizabeth, after being married many years, would have a baby. Their child would grow up to be John the Baptist, sent to make people ready for Jesus' coming.

A few months after Gabriel had visited Zechariah, he came to see Mary. The first chapter of Luke's Gospel tells us about it:

'In the sixth month of Elizabeth's pregnancy God sent the angel Gabriel to a town in Galilee named Nazareth. He had a message for a girl promised in marriage to a man named Joseph, who was a descendant of King David. The girl's name was Mary. The angel came to her and said, "Peace be with you! The Lord is with you and has greatly blessed you!"

Mary was deeply troubled by the angel's message, and she wondered what his words meant. The angel said to her, "Don't be afraid, Mary; God has been gracious to you. You will become pregnant and give birth to a son, and you will name him Jesus. He will be great and will be called the Son of the Most High God. The Lord God will make him a king, as his ancestor David was, and he will be the king of the descendants of Jacob for ever; his kingdom will never end!"'

When Jesus was born in Bethlehem, it was angels who brought the news to the shepherds in the nearby fields. They told the shepherds where to find the new baby.

CHURCH BELLS RING

Ding dong! merrily on high
in heaven the bells are ringing:
Ding dong! verily the sky
is riven with angel-singing:
Gloria, Hosanna in excelsis.

Before the days of radio, television or daily newspapers, church bells were used to send messages far and wide across the countryside. As well as calling people to church on Sundays, church bells were

rung to give news of special occasions such as victory in war or the birth of a prince. At Advent and Christmas, church bells still ring out from many churches to tell the good news of the birth of the King of kings.

In Scandinavia, church bells ring at four o'clock on Christmas Eve to let everyone know that the season of Christmas has begun and all work can stop. In many other countries the bells peal out at midnight, for it was once believed that midnight was the hour when Christ was born.

In one English church in Dewsbury, Yorkshire, a very different kind of ringing is heard each Christmas time. The great bell tolls slowly as if for a funeral. That is because it used to be said that when Jesus was born the Devil sickened and died. So this bell, called the Devil's Knell, is rung during the minutes before Christmas. On the stroke of midnight all the bells ring out in joyful sound. Christ is born — evil and sin are conquered.

A CHRISTMAS TREE ANGEL TO MAKE

You can make an angel — or a whole choir of them — to hang from your Christmas tree. This is how to do it.

Draw and cut out a disc, 4¾ in. in diameter, on colored paper — gold or silver look good.

2

From the center of the circle mark out three quarters of another circle, ¾ in. in diameter.

3

Mark lines A and B on the same diameter, 1 in. long.

4

Mark line C at right angles to lines A and B, from the outside of the disc to the inner circle.

Carefully cut along all the lines. A and B now become slots.

6

Without creasing the paper, wrap it round so that slot A slips into slot B. The angel's body now forms a cone.

7

Bend the head upright, and fix a piece of thread to the back of the head with tape, so that you can hang up the finished angel.

EVERYONE'S FAVOURITE SAINT

In the Middle Ages, St Nicholas was everyone's favourite saint. He was patron saint of all kinds of people, including merchants, sailors and small boys. Few facts are known about Nicholas, who was bishop of Myra, in Asia Minor, during the fourth century, but there are some very far-fetched legends about him. This one, the best known of all, may be true.

In Nicholas' home town, it is said, lived a family so poor that the father could not afford dowries for his three daughters. Nicholas determined to rescue them from starvation and distress, but without making his generosity known. So, when the eldest daughter was old enough to marry, he dropped a bag of gold in at her window by night. (Some say he

dropped it down the chimney, where it fell into the shoe or stocking she had left on the hearth to keep warm. And *that's* why children hang up their stocking or leave a shoe ready for presents.)

Nicholas did the same for the second and third daughters, but on the last occasion he was discovered by the grateful father. Nicholas swore him to secrecy. And that is why in some countries today, presents are given, especially to the children, on 5 December, which is St Nicholas' Eve.

ST NICHOLAS AND BLACK PETER IN HOLLAND

Every year, on the last Saturday in November, St Nicholas, dressed in bishop's robes and mitre, arrives by steamer at the port of Amsterdam, in Holland. With him is Black Peter, dressed in the costume of a Spaniard of the sixteenth century. St Nicholas disembarks, mounts a waiting white horse and rides off, accompanied by a jostling procession of children, first to the royal palace, where he is formally welcomed, then to his chosen headquarters for the season. Black Peter is supposed to be the Devil, now St Nicholas' servant, come to punish any naughty children, and to do the dirty work of taking presents down the chimneys.

Everyone in Holland gives presents on 5 December, St Nicholas' Eve, and every present should come as a surprise. Sometimes a tiny gift is wrapped in a huge box, or the parcel is hidden in an unexpected place — anything that makes it as much of a happy surprise as St Nicholas' first presents were said to be.

FATHER CHRISTMAS AND SANTA CLAUS

In the sixteenth century, after the Reformation, saints went out of favour in Europe. But someone was needed to take the place of St Nicholas and give presents at Christmas.

In England, a merry old character from children's plays, known as Father Christmas, took over the job.

France has Père Noel, and in Germany the Christkind, or Christ Child, gave gifts. In the United States, his name became Kris Kringle.

But Dutch settlers in America took St Nicholas with them. They shortened his name to Class and called him Sinta Class, which soon became Santa Claus in English. He became popular with everyone and American writers and artists gradually transformed the bishop in his robes and mitre into the familiar figure with white beard and robes and hat.

No one is sure how St Nicholas' white horse turned into a pack of reindeer. A nineteenth-century book shows a picture of him with just one reindeer and in 1882 Dr Clement Clarke Moore wrote a poem for his children about Santa Claus in which he described eight reindeer and gave them all names. But in Sweden he is still pictured drawn by mountain goats.

The English Father Christmas came to look more and more like his American counterpart, and now Father Christmas and Santa Claus have become one and the same person.

BISCUITS TO MAKE

On St Nicholas' Day, 6 December, Dutch children are given St Nicholas' letter biscuits to eat. This is how to make them.

You will need:
400g pastry/double-crust pastry
200g/8oz pack marzipan, a little milk
Also have ready:
a greased baking-sheet
rolling-pin
knife
pastry brush

1
Set the oven to 425° (Gas Regulo 7).

2
Roll the pastry out thinly. It is best to flour the board and rolling-pin lightly, to stop it sticking. Cut the pastry into strips about 10cms by 4cms.

3
Put a little sugar on your hands, then roll the marzipan into 'worms' about the thickness of your finger. Wrap each marzipan worm in a strip of pastry, gently pressing edges together with a dab of milk to join them.

4
Now gently form each roll into the shape of a letter. Some letters such as I, S or U are easy, so start with these. Others, like E, M or B will have to be made by using strips of different lengths and joining them (with milk for glue!).

5
Carefully place the completed letters on a baking-sheet, leaving space between each one. Bake for 10 to 15 minutes in the centre of the oven. Be very careful as you lift them off the tray. Don't worry if your letters don't look perfect — they'll taste good!

Christmas Comes to Narnia

by C.S. Lewis

In Narnia, the land on the other side of the magic wardrobe in C. S. Lewis' story, The Lion, the Witch and the Wardrobe, the children discover that it is always winter because of the spell of the wicked Witch — 'always winter, but never Christmas'. Then her evil power begins to weaken before the greater power of the Lion, Aslan. The children, hiding underground with their friends the beavers, suddenly hear a sound of jingling bells. Mr Beaver is the first to climb out of the cave to investigate . . .

'Come on!' cried Mr Beaver, who was almost dancing with delight. 'Come and see! This is a nasty knock for the Witch! It looks as if her power was already crumbling.'

'What *do* you mean, Mr Beaver?' panted Peter as they all scrambled up the steep bank of the valley together.

'Didn't I tell you,' answered Mr Beaver, 'that she'd made it always winter and never Christmas? Didn't I tell you? Well, just come and see!'

And then they were all at the top and did see.

It *was* a sledge, and it *was* reindeer with bells on their harness. But they were far bigger than the Witch's reindeer, and they were not white but brown. And on the sledge sat a person whom everyone knew the moment they set eyes on him. He was a huge man in a bright red robe (bright as holly-berries) with a hood that had fur inside it and a great white beard that fell like a foamy waterfall over his chest. Everyone knew him because, though you see people of his sort only in Narnia, you see pictures of them and hear them talked about even in our world — the world on this side of the wardrobe door. But when you really see them in Narnia it is rather different. Some of the pictures of Father Christmas in our world make him look only funny and jolly. But now that the children actually stood looking at him they didn't find it quite like that. He was so big, and so glad, and so real, that they all became quite still. They felt very glad, but also solemn.

'I've come at last,' said he. 'She has kept me out for a long time, but I have got in at last. Aslan is on the move. The Witch's magic is weakening.'

And Lucy felt running through her that deep shiver of gladness which you only get if you are being solemn and still.

'And now,' said Father Christmas, 'for your presents. There is a new and better sewing-machine for you, Mrs Beaver. I will drop it in your house as I pass.'

'If you please, sir', said Mrs Beaver, making a curtsey. 'It's locked up.'

'Locks and bolts make no difference to me,' said Father Christmas. 'And as for you, Mr Beaver, when you get home you will find your dam finished and mended and all the leaks stopped and a new sluice-gate fitted.'

Mr Beaver was so pleased that he opened his mouth very wide and then found he couldn't say anything at all.

'Peter, Adam's Son', said Father Christmas.

'Here, sir,' said Peter.

'These are your presents,' was the answer, 'and they are tools not toys. The time to use them is perhaps near at hand. Bear them well.' With these words he handed to Peter a shield and a sword. The shield was the colour of silver and across it there ramped a red lion, as bright as a ripe strawberry at the moment when you pick it. The hilt of the sword was of gold and it had a sheath and a sword belt and everything it needed, and it was just the right size and weight for Peter to use. Peter was silent and solemn as he received these gifts, for he felt they were a very serious kind of present.

'Susan, Eve's Daughter,' said Father Christmas. 'These are for you,' and he handed her a bow and a quiver full of arrows and a little ivory horn. 'You must use the bow only in great need,' he said, 'for I do not mean you to fight in the battle. It does not easily miss. And when you put this horn to your lips and blow it, then, wherever you are, I think help of some kind will come to you.'

Last of all he said, 'Lucy, Eve's Daughter,' and Lucy came forward. He gave her a little bottle of what looked like glass (but people said

afterwards that it was made of diamond) and a small dagger. 'In this bottle,' he said, 'there is a cordial made of the juice of one of the fire-flowers that grow in the mountains of the sun. If you or any of your friends is hurt, a few drops of this will restore them. And the dagger is to defend yourself at great need. For you also are not to be in the battle.'

'Why, sir?' said Lucy. 'I think — I don't know — but I think I could be brave enough.'

'That is not the point,' he said. 'But battles are ugly when women fight. And now' — here he suddenly looked less grave — 'here is something for the moment for you all!' and he brought out (I suppose from the big bag at his back, but nobody quite saw him do it) a large tray containing five cups and saucers, a bowl of lump sugar, a jug of cream, and a great big teapot all sizzling and piping hot. Then he cried out 'Merry Christmas! Long live the true King!' and cracked his whip, and he and the reindeer and the sledge and all were out of sight before anyone realized that they had started.

PRESENTS TO GIVE

Giving presents is just as much fun as getting them, and people have always enjoyed exchanging presents at this time of year. But it is God's wonderful present to us at the first Christmas that gives Christmas present giving its real meaning.

St John tells us that God loved us so much that he gave us Jesus, his Son. When St Paul thought about that most wonderful of all presents he exclaimed, 'Let us thank God for his priceless gift.'

God's present to us was an expensive one: it cost him a lot. When we talk about expensive presents we often think only of how much money they cost. But presents which cost us time, thought and trouble are often even more valuable. So it's a good idea to make as many of your presents as you can.

Here are a few ideas for presents that are both easy and inexpensive to make; presents to suit almost anyone — dads and uncles, mums and aunts, brothers and sisters, or friends.

KEY TIDY

Decorate a wooden spoon, using paints or felt-tipped pens or designs cut out of sticky-backed plastic. Ask a grown-up to make several holes along the handle of the spoon, then screw in some cup-hooks. Add a loop of cord for the key tidy to hang by.

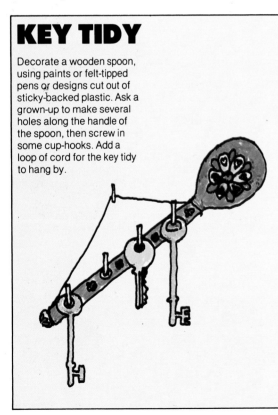

CALENDARS

Here are two basic ideas for wall calendars which you can adapt to suit your own ideas and the materials you have to hand.

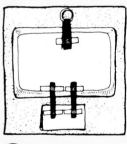

1
Paint the rim of a round cheesebox (the kind that holds wrapped cheese portions). Stick a circle of felt in the centre. Arrange a design of dried flowers, cones or seedheads on the felt and stick them on with rubber solution glue.

2
A polystyrene meat-tray (wiped clean) makes an unusual calendar. Arrange a design made from short macaroni and long spaghetti and other shaped pasta. Stick with rubber-based glue. Paint thickly. On the back of both these calendars stick a loop of ribbon holding a brass ring for hanging. Use sticky tape to join two short lengths of ribbon on to a pocket calendar.

ODDS-AND-ENDS BOX

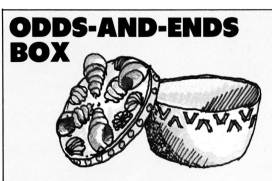

Many soft margarine containers are attractively decorated already. They make useful boxes for anything from paper clips to peanuts! You will need to cover the trade name on the lid. Here are two suggested ways.

1

Draw round the lid onto a piece of colourful felt. Cut out the circle and stick it on to the lid. Add a length of lace round the edge, or stick an unusual button in the centre.

2

Cover the lid with polyfilla paste and arrange attractive stone or shells or dried flowers or seed-heads in the paste while it is still soft.

NO-COOKING SWEETS

You will need:
225g/2 cups icing sugar
1 egg white
flavouring and colouring

1

Sieve the icing sugar into a bowl. Carefully separate the white from the yolk of the egg (you will not need the yolk).

2

Beat the egg white, then pour slowly into the icing sugar.

3

Blend with a knife, then knead until well mixed.

4

Roll into small balls and flatten the tops. Leave on an icing-sugared plate to harden.

For **strawberry creams** add three drops of strawberry essence and three of red colouring with the egg white. **Coffee creams** need one teaspoonful of coffee essence.
To make **almond creams** add three drops of almond essence and green colouring.
Peppermint creams can also be green, or left white. They need three drops of peppermint essence.

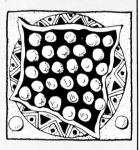

Chi-Wee's Special Present

by Grace P. Moon

Inside the Indian trading store, Chi-Wee saw her mother stroke a beautiful, soft wool shawl. It was dark blue on one side and glowing red on the other, with a fringe of the same two colours. Chi-Wee saw the look of longing in her mother's eyes.

'My Mother, you will buy this beautiful shawl?' she asked.

'No, my little one. This day the pottery I have made must be traded for food only.'

'But you need a warm shawl,' cried Chi-Wee. 'The wind is cold! You need this shawl!'

'We will not speak of it more, my daughter,' said her mother.

Chi-Wee stood looking at the bright-coloured shawl. In her heart a fierce little voice said, 'My mother shall have that shawl. The "Good Spirit" made that shawl to be for my mother.'

The shawl cost six dollars, and there were few ways for a little Indian girl of that time to earn so much money. Yet over and over again, Chi-Wee imagined putting that wonderful shawl around the shoulders of her mother.

When next they went to the trading post, Chi-Wee, with trembling fingers, thrust a pink shell necklace into the hands of the man who ran the store. It was her most precious possession!

'I know this is not enough, but could you . . . Oh, could you please keep this shawl for me?' Chi-Wee pleaded. 'It's for my mother. I will pay more on it the next time.'

The expression in the eyes of the trader softened, and a faraway look appeared in his eyes as he said tenderly, 'If she had lived, my daughter would be about your age. Yes, I will keep this shawl for you, little girl of the mesa, until you bring the rest of the money.'

The following month was a very busy one for Chi-Wee. She could hardly wait for the next trading day to come, and her eyes shone with pride when she handed the trader a great jar of wild honey. Chi-Wee did not tell him of the many days of hard labour she had had in gathering it, or of the painful lumps on her arms that told of the angry stinging of the bees.

There was a look she could not understand in the eyes of the trader. 'I hope you won't mind, the bright-coloured shawl is gone. But I

22

have other beautiful shawls, little girl,' he said.

Chi-Wee could not speak; words would not come. Her eyes filled with tears as she ran from the store. She slumped sadly in the wagon while her mother finished her purchases. All the way home in the bumpety old wagon there was a storm of anger and grief in Chi-Wee's heart. 'It cannot be true,' she thought. 'People cannot be so thoughtless and cruel.'

When they arrived home, Chi-Wee's mother called her to help unload the parcels.

'And here's one, Chi-Wee, that the trader said you had bought. With what could you buy it, my daughter?'

Chi-Wee did not wait to answer. She tore open the paper of the parcel. It was the shawl — that wonderful shawl for her mother! Tied to one corner was a note that said, 'It is the love for your mother that has bought this shawl, little girl of the mesa; and it is my love for another little girl like you that gives back your precious treasure.'

Chi-Wee looked, and there, pinned to the shawl, was her pink-shell necklace.

Tears of happiness and gratitude glistened in Chi-Wee's eyes as she wrapped the beautiful bright-coloured shawl around her mother's shoulders.

Chi-Wee had learned a great secret: when we love and truly want to give, the 'Good Spirit' opens the way to our heart's desire.

Piccola

by Mala Powers

Little Piccola's heart was always warm and cheerful. Lovingly she sang as she helped her mother in their stone cottage.

She scoured the pots and pans, and she tended the geraniums that bloomed in the windows. She dragged in great armfuls of wood for the fire, made the fire, and scrubbed the floors.

'My Piccola is busy as the bee,' said her mother.

'My Piccola is joyous as the lark,' said her father.

Piccola brought laughter to the family, even through the many long winter evenings when none of them had had quite enough to eat.

Hard times had come to the family in their

24

small French village by the seacoast. Piccola's father, a fisherman, had been very ill and could not go to sea, and her mother struggled to feed her family through that long, hard winter. In spite of all the hardships, Piccola's faith remained always strong.

'Spring will soon come for us,' she would say, 'and summer, too; and then, dear Papa, you will be well and strong again.'

As the weeks slipped by and the little family's store of money grew smaller and smaller, Piccola's laughter still rang through their cottage; and when the holidays came, she cried out, 'Oh, how I do love Christmas!'

'Dearest Piccola,' said her father sadly, 'you must know that this year we are so poor that we cannot have even a single gift for you.'

Piccola heard what he said, but did not doubt at all that something beautiful must befall each and every child upon the Christmas Day.

On the night before Christmas, after Piccola had finished her work, she seized her father and mother by the hands.

'Let us go out and share in the Christmas joy!' she pleaded.

So they left their own small, dark cottage and went out into the village. Throughout the village and in each cottage, all the windows were decorated for Christmas and ablaze with candlelight. So close to the streets were the little stone houses, that, in each one, Piccola and her mother and father could see and hear the happiness and Christmas cheer within.

'Every house but ours is joyous,' sighed the father.

But Piccola did not even hear him. She was laughing, and her eyes sparkled with joy. 'How rich we are,' she said, 'for all the ornaments and cheer in each door and window are ours to enjoy!'

When at last they returned to their little cottage, Piccola kissed her parents goodnight and said, 'Now I shall set out my shoe for my Christmas gift.'

'Oh, Piccola,' cried her mother, almost in tears, 'there can be no gift for you this year.' Even so, Piccola's small wooden shoe was set by the fireplace, and they all went off to bed.

Full of faith as always, Piccola awoke with the grey dawn and crept quietly to the fireplace

to look into the shoe for her Christmas gift.

'Father! Mother! Come quickly!' she cried. 'Look! See what the good Saint Nicholas has brought!' And there in Piccola's little wooden shoe was a tiny shivering baby bird.

'It probably fell out of its nest and down the chimney into her shoe,' remarked her father.

Piccola paid no heed. The baby bird had come as her Christmas gift! She knew! And her joy was so full, as she cuddled and warmed and fed the tiny bird, that soon her father and mother caught her joyful spirit, and they were warmed and became happy too.

So, Christmas came to Piccola, rich and full, because the spirit of Christmas was always in her heart!

St Lucy's Day in Sweden

*Now light one thousand Christmas lights
On dark earth here tonight,
One thousand thousand also shine
To make the dark sky bright.*

FROM A SWEDISH CAROL

From time immemorial the people of Sweden have kept 13 December — 'the day when the sun stands still' — as a festival of light. They knew that after this darkest day of the year (as it once was) the sun would return and the days lengthen.

When monks brought the gospel to Sweden they told the story of St Lucia, a Christian girl under the bitter persecution of the Roman Emperor Diocletian. Some legends say that she brought food to Christians hiding in the catacombs of Rome, wearing lights on her head to leave her hands free. So the pagan festival of light was transformed into the feast of St Lucy, held also on 13th December.

Early in the morning the girl chosen as Lucy, one of the daughters in the family, steals quietly from bed and dresses in a white gown with red sash. She arranges a crown of green leaves on her head to which are attached five tall white candles. Today electric candles are most often used, for safety. With great care St Lucy carries a tray of coffee and saffron buns to the rest of the family still snug in bed. She usually sings them a special song about the coming of St Lucy.

Towns and villages, schools, offices and factories, have their own St Lucy and there is also an official one. She visits hospitals and children's homes.

Swedish settlers have taken their St Lucy customs to the USA.

'LIGHT HAS COME INTO THE WORLD'

'God . . . will cause the bright dawn of salvation to rise on us and to shine from heaven on all those who live in the dark shadow of death.' That is how Zechariah described the first

PEPPARKAKOR BISCUITS

Swedish ginger snaps, called pepparkakor, are favourites at Christmas, hung on the Christmas tree or added to the St Lucy breakfast trays. If you want to hang some on the tree you can make a small hole in one corner of the dough before cooking, or pierce after cooking, before the biscuits harden. Then thread through with needle and cotton.

You will need:
400g/3 cups sifted flour
1 teaspoon bicarbonate of soda
1 ½ teaspoons of ground ginger,
ground cloves and cinnamon
230g/1 cup butter or margarine
230g/1 cup dark brown sugar
2 egg whites

1 Sift flour, spices and soda.

2 Cream butter and sugar until very fluffy then beat in egg whites. Slowly work in dry ingredients.

3 Wrap and chill for 12 hours.

4 Heat oven to 350°C (Gas Regulo 4).

5 Roll out dough to ½cm thick on lightly floured board. Cut into as many fancy shapes as you have different cutters. Place on ungreased baking-sheet, leaving space between.

6 Cook for 10-12 minutes until light brown round edge. Cool on wire racks.

7 Prepare icing while biscuits cool. Blend icing sugar (about 250g/1 cup) with 1 egg white. Make it stiff enough to pipe, in your own chosen patterns, on to biscuits.

Christmas. Like other Bible writers he pictured Jesus' coming as bright light in a dark world. Christmas tree lights, street decorations, stars, candles and lanterns still remind us of that light today.

In **Sweden** during the four Sundays of Advent a candle is lit each Sunday. They stand in a special Advent candlestick holding four candles. A special star with an electric light in it is put up in a window. It is called the Advent star.

In **Norway** families light a candle every evening from Christmas Eve until New Year.

In **S India** Christians fill little clay lamps with oil, putting a piece of twisted cotton in each for a wick. When night comes, they put the lighted lamps along the edge of their low, flat-roofed houses. Neighbours, who do not know the Christmas story, ask them why they have lights at that time of year and they explain that Jesus has come and brought them light.

In **Mexico** bonfires are lit and fireworks let off into the blackness of the night after the midnight service on Christmas Eve is over.

THE CHRISTMAS TREE

How did it all begin? No one really knows, though the custom of having Christmas trees certainly comes from Germany. At one time 'Adam and Eve Day' was celebrated on 24 December. They decorated a tree, known as the Paradise Tree, with apples and fruit. And they acted the story of the Garden of Eden and how, in the beginning, the world was spoilt.

A legend links the Christmas tree with St Boniface of Crediton, who left England to bring the good news about Jesus to the tribes of Germany. One dark night he and his monks came upon a group of villagers preparing to sacrifice a boy to their god, Odin. They had tied him to an oak tree. Boniface set the boy free and chopped the oak tree down. He pointed instead to an evergreen fir and his followers stepped forward and put their candles on its branches. By its light, the people listened as Boniface told them of a loving God who had brought life and light to the world through his Son.

Some say it was Martin Luther, the great sixteenth-century reformer, who first brought the lighted Christmas tree indoors. As he walked through the forest one night he looked up to see the stars shining through the branches. It was so beautiful he went home to tell his children how the lighted tree was like a picture of Jesus, who left the starry heaven to bring light to earth.

DECORATING THE TREE

At first, Christmas trees were decorated with things to eat — edible angels, gingerbread men and apples. German glass-blowers may have been the first to make glass ornaments which were not so heavy. At first a little model of baby Jesus was put at the top of the tree. This changed to an angel with gold wings; then to the fairy we see on so many Christmas trees today!

Candles were used to light the tree at first, and there were many bad accidents from fire. In 1895 an American telephone worker, Ralph Morris, thought how good the tiny light bulbs on the switchboard would look on his tree! His inspiration led to the many shapes and colours of electric Christmas tree lights manufactured today.

SPECIAL CHRISTMAS TREES

Many towns have their own Christmas tree, set up in the square or high street. One of the best-known stands in Trafalgar Square in London. Every December a magnificent fir tree is shipped over from Oslo in Norway as a present from the people of Norway, in gratitude for the help given to them by Britain in the second world war.

Since the 1920s there has been a large Christmas tree on the White House lawn in Washington. The President himself switches on the lights.

In New Zealand the Christmas tree is alive and growing. Its Maori name is Pohutakawa, but early settlers called it the Christmas tree because its beautiful red flowers bloom in December. The huge trees grow mostly by lake and sea side and holiday-makers can tread a carpet of its red stamens down to the water's edge.

THE ROYAL CHRISTMAS TREE

It was Prince Albert, Queen Victoria's German husband, who made the Christmas tree popular in Britain. In 1841 he wrote to his father:

'Today I have two children of my own . . . who . . . are full of happy wonder at the German Christmas tree and its radiant candles.'

In 1848 The Illustrated London News *described the royal tree as, 'About eight feet tall . . . On each branch are arranged a dozen wax tapers . . . Fancy cakes, gilt gingerbread and eggs filled with sweetmeats, are also suspended by variously-coloured ribbons from the branches . . . The tree . . . is supported at the root by piles of sweets of a larger kind, and by toys and dolls of all descriptions, suited to the . . . ages of . . . Royalty for whose gratification they are displayed.'*

The Santa Claus of Kanimbla Valley

by Bernard O'Reilly

Herbert went away north to join Tom. There they worked for two years in the canefields and the copper mines, earning money that was badly needed at home. The Christmas before they returned was a hard one; money was very scarce. Norbert, too was working away. Two days before Christmas — yes, in the middle of summer, cold rain began to stream down and snow fell on the mountains! On Christmas Eve the downfall continued and quite early in the morning a great roar from the granite gorge beyond Marsden's Rock, told that Cox's River, in one of its bursts of fury was coming down with a solid wall of water twenty feet deep; the Cox nearly always came down that way, and faster than a man could run.

We were cut off from the Blue Mountains and the shop in Blackheath where our slender Christmas order had been placed. It was a grey,

terrible day, a sodden earth and a sodden sky, and always the steady, cold rain, and always Cox's River roaring like the maddened monster that it was. Mother was ill, it was shortly before Joe was born; is there anything more sad or desolate than a home with a sick mother?

Tom had once swum the Cox in flood like that, after a cloudburst, with inches of hail floating on top, and racing logs, bigger than tiger sharks and just as dangerous. But Tom was beyond Cloncurry, nearly 2,000 miles away. Night came on, and the family faced a cheerless Christmas; there would be none of those little luxuries which helped to make the Holy Day the happiest day of the year for bush people. Worse still, there were three little ones with implicit faith in Santa Claus, and three expectant stockings hung at the foot of a bed. It was almost the identical setting of Bret Harte's

immortal Christmas story, 'How Santa Claus came to Simpson's Bar,' but in our case there was no big, reckless, half-drunken miner who faced a double death and a double temptation, so that a child's stocking might not be empty on Christmas morning.

Our story worked out in a different way. Molly, who had herself not long outgrown Santa Claus, could not bear the thought of those empty stockings. All night long she worked by the light of a smoky oil lamp, painting rainbow colours on old, worn, rubber balls, fashioning little toys and covering them with silver paper, making necklaces and bracelets with bright beads taken from milk-jug covers, making toffee and parcelling it up in coloured paper. With the chill, wet dawn, three young people

awakened to find stockings fat with mysterious parcels, and not all the toys of a millionaire's child could have made them happier that Christmas morning.

A week later, when the flats dried up and the river subsided, someone 'found' a mysterious parcel of toys which must surely have been accidentally dropped from Santa's chariot. They were nice toys and we liked them, but none thought half as much of them as of those which came on Christmas Day.

CHRISTMAS CARDS

If you had been at school in England some hundred and fifty years ago, you would have been busy preparing your 'Christmas piece'. Each pupil was given a piece of paper with special heading and borders on which to write Christmas greetings to his family in best copper-plate writing. There were no such things as Christmas cards then.

Sir Henry Cole, a civil servant concerned with Post Office reform, was probably the first to have the idea of the Christmas card. And his artist friend, John Horsley, designed one for Christmas 1843 which sold at one shilling — a lot of money.

A specially engraved card, made by young William Egley at about the same time, is now in the British Museum.

But the idea did not catch on at first. Cards only became popular when newly invented methods of printing and reduced postal rates made them far cheaper to buy and send. By the end of the century cards were being made cheaply all over Europe, especially in Germany. An enterprising printer in Boston, Louis Prang, had already been making cards showing scenes of Jesus' birth.

ROBINS AND STAGE COACHES

The robin, with his scarlet breast, is a frequent visitor to English gardens in winter, and there are plenty to be seen on Christmas cards too. Some people explain their popularity on the first cards by the fact that Victorian postmen were called Robin Postmen because of their red-trimmed uniform. They delivered the first cards.

In 1836 — before Christmas cards — there was a terrible snowstorm in England and mail coaches with the Christmas mail were held up or caught in drifts. Memories of that dreadful Christmas lingered on and that may account for the number of cards with scenes of stage coaches in the snow that have appeared right up to this very day.

NOVELTY CARDS

Christmas cards soon came to be made in all kinds of fancy designs. Some were in the shape of fans, stars or half-moons, studded with 'jewels'. Hand-made cards are the nicest to receive and you could

make unusual, decorated ones yourself. The wise men, in rich robes, with glittering gifts would make a good picture.

To make the cards you could use scraps of foil, velvet, knitting-wool, ribbon, glue, 'glitter', 'snow', cotton wool. Small beads and buttons could be used on cards not to be sent through the post.

CARDS TO HELP OTHERS

Look out for cards sold in aid of good causes. Profits go direct to the charity named. By buying these you wish your friends a happy Christmas *and* help to bring happiness to people in great need.

CHRISTMAS SEALS

At the beginning of this century, a Danish Post Office worker was busy stamping Christmas letters and cards when a splendid idea struck him. Why not print seals to decorate and brighten envelopes and at the same time swell funds for sufferers from tuberculosis, a 'killer'

disease very common at that time.

His idea was a great success. More than four million seals were sold the first year they were produced. Sweden adopted the idea that same year and Norway two years later. Many countries today sell Christmas seals in aid of favourite good causes.

POST EARLY FOR CHRISTMAS

You could volunteer to be Robin Postman for any neighbour who can't get out to post or might find postage too expensive for local cards. Work out your route first, so that you don't

retrace your steps too many times.

Schools, churches and youth groups sometimes have a post-box of their own, where cards can be posted for friends who also attend.

There's a grand opening ceremony just before Christmas. You can make a post-box from an empty supermarket cardboard carton.

1
Stand carton on end.

2
Cut slot in side (150mm × 50mm).

3
Sticky-tape all open sides and end.

4
Make a parcel by wrapping securely in red crepe paper.

5
Cut diagonally across slot, and fold inwards. Secure on the inside with sticky-tape.

6
Glue cotton wool over top.

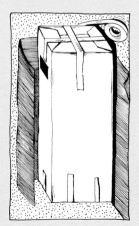
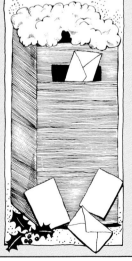

St Thomas and Christingle

Christmas is coming, the goose is getting fat,
Please to put a penny in the old man's hat.
If you haven't got a penny a ha'penny will do,
If you haven't got a ha'penny a farthing will do,
If you haven't got a farthing — God bless you!

St Thomas was made the patron saint of old people — and of children too. In days gone by, old and young were allowed to go round collecting money on 21 December, which is St Thomas' Day, to buy food for their Christmas dinners. The custom was called a-Thomasing, or else a-mumping or a-gooding!

The children would give a sprig of holly or mistletoe to anyone who put money in their collecting-box. St Thomas' Day was often a school holiday, but if they did have to go to school, children made it a day for tricks against the teacher. Sometimes they would lock him out of school and get up to all kinds of fun and games inside on their own.

Two hundred years ago in 1785, Parson James Woodforde wrote in his diary:

'This being St Thomas' Day, had a great many Poor People of the Parish to visit me, I gave to each of them that came, sixpence'.

One hundred years ago in 1886, the people of Brighton, on the south coast of England, collected money for the old people of the town and held a special ceremony in the police court to distribute it. A report said, 'The oldest of them all, the lady of 96, came into the court despite the sharpness of the wind and the frozen roads.'

Christmas is still the time to remember and help the very old and the very young. Here are some suggestions:

★ Visit anyone elderly or housebound who may need shopping done for them before Christmas.
★ Invite someone who has no family near to share your family Christmas meal.
★ Give to any central collection of tinned foods set up by local social services.
★ Contribute toys, books or money at a special church service.

THE CHRISTINGLE SERVICE

One way to help families with special needs is to take part in a Christingle service. The ceremony is very old. No one knows just how far back it goes. There are records of an ancient Welsh 'calenig' service, and the Moravian church has held Christingle services for over two hundred years, though they do not believe that the custom began with them.

About fifteen years ago, John Pensom, of the Church of England Children's Society in Britain, revived the custom and in 1982 over a thousand services were held in many countries. More than £100,000 was collected to help handicapped children, those without homes, and families in need. Christingle means Christ-Light, and the service is a celebration of the coming of Christ, the Light, into the world. At the service, gifts of money, collected beforehand, are presented and, in turn, Christingles are received.

When all the Christingles have been given out, carols are sung by the candlelight.

MAKING A CHRISTINGLE

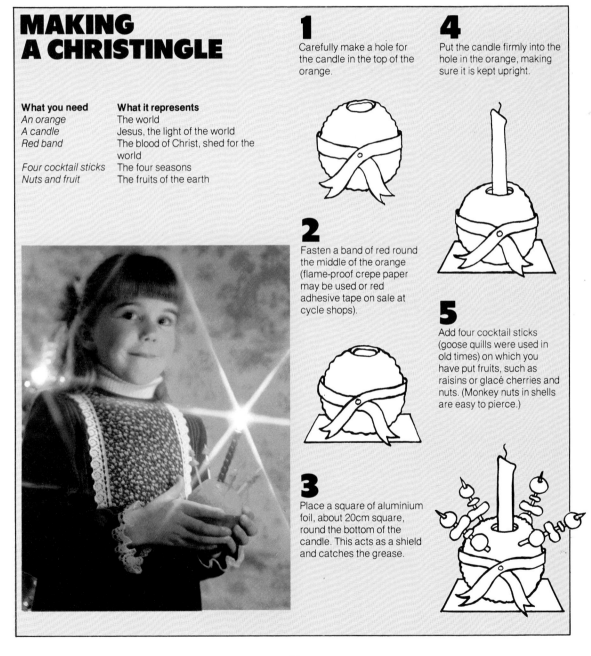

What you need

What you need	What it represents
An orange	The world
A candle	Jesus, the light of the world
Red band	The blood of Christ, shed for the world
Four cocktail sticks	The four seasons
Nuts and fruit	The fruits of the earth

1 Carefully make a hole for the candle in the top of the orange.

2 Fasten a band of red round the middle of the orange (flame-proof crepe paper may be used or red adhesive tape on sale at cycle shops).

3 Place a square of aluminium foil, about 20cm square, round the bottom of the candle. This acts as a shield and catches the grease.

4 Put the candle firmly into the hole in the orange, making sure it is kept upright.

5 Add four cocktail sticks (goose quills were used in old times) on which you have put fruits, such as raisins or glacé cherries and nuts. (Monkey nuts in shells are easy to pierce.)

Little Women at Christmas

by Louisa M. Alcott

It was a hundred years ago when Louisa M. Alcott was asked to write a book for girls and began one which was really about her own family of sisters when they were young. She herself was Jo. The story of Little Women *begins one Christmas when their father is away at the Civil War and money is short. 'Christmas won't be Christmas without any presents!' Jo complains. But they soon devise a scheme for buying surprise presents for their mother — Marmee — with the dollar each has saved. On Christmas morning, breakfast is ready and waiting and the little basket of presents awaits Mrs March's arrival. She has been out visiting in response to a call for help. At last she returns . . .*

Another bang of the street door sent the basket under the sofa, and the girls to the table, eager for breakfast.

'Merry Christmas, Marmee! Many of them! Thank you for our books; we read some, and mean to every day,' they cried, in chorus.

'Merry Christmas, little daughters! I'm glad you began at once, and hope you will keep on. But I want to say one word before we sit down. Not far away from here lies a poor woman with a little new-born baby. Six children are huddled into one bed to keep from freezing, for they have no fire. There is nothing to eat over there; and the oldest boy came to tell me they were suffering hunger and cold. My girls, will you give them your breakfast as a Christmas present?'

They were all unusually hungry, having waited nearly an hour, and for a minute no one spoke; only a minute, for Jo exclaimed impetuously,

'I'm so glad you came before we began!'

'May I go and help carry the things to the poor little children?' asked Beth eagerly.

'I shall take the cream and the muffins,' added Amy, heroically giving up the articles she most liked.

Meg was already covering the buckwheats, and piling the bread into one big plate.

'I thought you'd do it,' said Mrs March, smiling as if satisfied. 'You shall all go and help me, and when we come back we will have bread and milk for breakfast, and make it up at dinner time.'

They were soon ready, and the procession set out. Fortunately it was early, and they went through back streets, so few people saw them, and no one laughed at the queer party.

A poor, bare, miserable room it was, with broken windows, no fire, ragged bed-clothes, a sick mother, wailing baby, and a group of pale, hungry children cuddled under one old quilt, trying to keep warm.

How the big eyes stared, and the blue lips smiled, as the girls went in!

'Ach, mein Gott! it is good angels come to us!' said the poor woman, crying for joy.

'Funny angels in hoods and mittens,' said Jo, and set them laughing.

In a few minutes it really did seem as if kind spirits had been at work there. Hannah, who had carried wood, made a fire, and stopped up the broken panes with old hats and her own cloak. Mrs March gave the mother tea and gruel, and comforted her with promises of help, while she dressed the little baby as tenderly as if it had been her own. The girls, meantime, spread the table, set the children round the fire, and fed them like so many hungry birds; laughing, talking, and trying to understand the funny broken English.

'Das ist gut!' 'Die Engel-kinder!' cried the poor things, as they ate, and warmed their purple hands at the comfortable blaze.

The girls had never been called angel children before, and thought it very agreeable, especially Jo, who had been considered a 'Sancho' ever since she was born. That was a very happy breakfast, though they didn't get any of it; and when they went away, leaving comfort behind, I think there were not in all the city four merrier people than the hungry little girls who gave away their breakfasts, and contented themselves with bread and milk on Christmas morning.

DECORATIONS

Long before the days of Christian Christmas, people gathered evergreens in December and decorated their homes and temples, to drive away evil spirits and remind them that spring would soon come with new green growth. Some early Christian leaders disapproved of carrying on this heathen custom, but others wanted to continue, giving it Christian meaning. Their view carried the day. In the fifteenth century one writer noted that in London, 'Every house and every parish church is decked with holm, ivy, bays . . . whatever is green.'

Holly, once called holm, was given all kinds of Christian associations. Some told the story that a holly tree stood, bare of berries, which the birds had eaten, outside the stable where Christ was born. In honour of Christ's birth, the tree straightaway bore buds, flowers and berries, all in one night! In the carol, 'The Holly and the Ivy', the prickly holly leaves are a picture of Christ's crown of thorns and the red berries of his blood shed for us.

Holly is easy to grow. We have two small trees in our garden, accidently 'sown' by birds who had eaten berries. If your holly branches have no berries for Christmas — they never do in Australia and New Zealand, where Christmas comes in summer — then you can cheat by wiring on some plastic berries on sale in some florist shops.

Mistletoe has a place in the folklore of many countries and was part of pagan New Year ceremonies among the druids in Britain. Some say it was banned from church for that reason, but many church accounts in England in the Middle Ages show payments for mistletoe to be used to decorate the church at Christmas. In York Minster there was a special mistletoe ceremony, where wrongdoers in the city could come to receive a pardon. In England mistletoe is also linked with kissing. An unwary girl can be kissed under a sprig of mistletoe hanging up in the house. In old times, a berry had to be plucked and given to each girl kissed. When all the berries had gone the kissing had to stop!

Rosemary is often grown today in gardens, to be used in cooking or for beauty care. It used to be a favourite decoration because of its attractive green spikes and fragrant smell.

THE YULE LOG

As well as branches of evergreen, a great log was brought into the house at Yule time, and this custom continued in Christian times too. Different kinds of wood were chosen in different countries of Europe. Oak, ash, pine and olive were the favourites, and birch was used in Scotland. The log was stripped of its bark and dragged in amid great rejoicing and special ceremony. Since it was to burn for the whole twelve days of Christmas it had to be very large, filling the whole family hearth. It had to be lighted from a stump left from last year's log.

A LOG WITH COLOURED FLAMES

If you have an open fire suitable for burning wood, you might like to prepare a special yule log, which will burn with different coloured flames. You will need the following chemicals:

Chemical	Colour of flame	Where to obtain
Potassium nitrate	Violet	Chemistry set or chemical suppliers
Barium nitrate	Apple green	As above
Borax	Vivid green	Chemist shops
Copper sulphate	Blue	Garden centres
Table salt	Yellow	In the kitchen!

Mix each chemical in turn with some shellac, to make a paste. Paint small patches onto the log. Or you can mix chemical and shellac with sawdust, drill small holes in the log, and fill it with the mixture. You might be allowed to prepare a yule log in woodwork and chemistry classes near the end of term at school.

CHRISTMAS TABLE DECORATIONS

In Sweden, many decorations are home made. Christmas goats, all different sizes, are made from straw. Here are two Christmas table decorations for you to make.

You will need:
Piece of wood or small log
Candle
Holly or evergreen
Tube of glitter
Nail or glue
Plasticene

1
Find a suitable flat piece of wood or small log from forest or woods.

2
Hammer nail through wood from underneath, taking care to keep your hand clear, and fix to candle in the chosen position.

3
Press plasticene on to wood.

4
Arrange small pieces of evergreens and baubles, pushing stems into plasticene to grip well. If you want a pretty glittering effect when the candle is lit, daub a little glue on to evergreen leaves and dust with glitter. Finish with a red bow if desired.

CAROLS

One of the pleasures of Christmas is singing carols. The carols in this book, from different countries, are only a few of the many carols that have been written down the ages.

It was only a few hundred years after Jesus' birth that learned archbishops first began writing solemn hymns about the Christmas story. But it was during the fifteenth century that carols belonging to the ordinary people became popular all over Europe.

Many people think that 'carol' comes from a word meaning to dance, so the tunes that set your feet tapping are often the old sing-and-dance carols of long ago. Later these carols were frowned upon, despised and almost

forgotten for a few hundred years, for no one had written down words or music. But they lived on in the memories of country folk, who went on singing them, and in the nineteenth century a new interest in them sprang up. They were carefully listened to, written down and collected into hymn books to be placed alongside the splendid Christmas hymns of Wesley in Britain and Luther in Germany. So today we have carols to suit all moods and occasions.

MIXED LANGUAGE CAROLS

For many hundreds of years Latin was the language used in

church. Some of the first Christian hymns were written in Latin. Folk carols often mixed in a few Latin words or phrases with their own language. The German carol, *In Dulci Jubilo* is one example of these mixed language carols which have the strange name macaronic.

CAROL SINGING

In **England,** many churches have a service of Bible readings interspersed with carols. They follow the famous Festival of Nine Lessons and Carols held every Christmas Eve in the chapel of King's College, Cambridge. This service has been heard over the air ever since broadcasting began. Now it is televised too and has become a traditional part of Christmas listening and viewing.

In the **United States,** in Jackson Square, New Orleans, thousands of carollers gather on 22 December for community carol singing. And in Boston singers and hand-bell players celebrate on Beacon Hill.

Every morning from 16 December to Christmas Eve, a special mass is celebrated in the churches of **Puerto Rico.** Lively happy carols take the place of hymns and workers leave church to go about their usual business still cheerfully singing carols.

The Song from Heaven

Everyone was singing it. The King of Prussia heard it and was so impressed that he ordered it to be sung every Christmas in his cathedral. But where had the carol come from? No one knew. Some said it was so beautiful that it must have been sent straight from God, without needing a human author. They called it *The Song from Heaven.*

It all began in the Austrian village of Oberndorf, some eleven miles from Salzburg. Joseph Mohr, who was assistant priest at the church of St Nicholas, determined to provide something special for his congregation at the midnight Christmas service. He wanted to make up for the fact that the organ had broken down. The church lay so close to the river that damp and rust had affected the organ and his good friend, Franz Gruber, could not squeeze a note out of it.

So on Christmas Eve 1818 Joseph sat down and wrote:

Silent night, holy night!
Sleeps the world; hid from sight,
Mary and Joseph in stable bare
Watch o'er the child beloved and fair,
Sleeping in heavenly rest.

He finished the poem and sent it post haste to Gruber, asking him to set it to music ready for that night. They would sing it together, using a guitar for accompaniment. Gruber got to work quickly and wrote the tune in a couple of hours, giving him time to practise it with the choir before midnight arrived. That self-same night the people of Oberndorf listened as Mohr and Gruber sang, the choir repeating the last lines in full harmony.

Christmas passed, spring came and an organ builder arrived to do repairs. Perhaps a copy of *Silent Night* still lay in the cupboard, for he found it and was delighted by it. As he travelled around, mending and building organs, he took the carol with him.

Two strolling families of singers heard it and made it part of their repertoire. One family performed it before the King of Prussia, while the other travelled as far as the United States, making the carol famous there.

The Song from Heaven, written by an unknown poet and musician in a single day, became the carol still sung and loved at Christmas time all over the world.

CHRISTMAS IN THE SUN

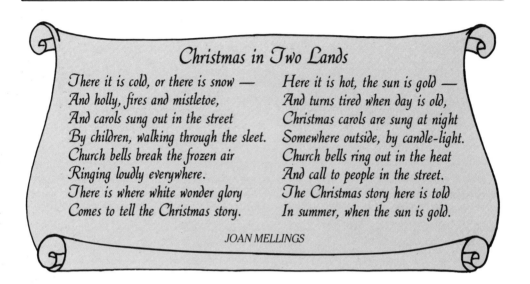

Christmas in Two Lands

There it is cold, or there is snow —
And holly, fires and mistletoe,
And carols sung out in the street
By children, walking through the sleet.
Church bells break the frozen air
Ringing loudly everywhere.
There is where white wonder glory
Comes to tell the Christmas story.

Here it is hot, the sun is gold —
And turns tired when day is old,
Christmas carols are sung at night
Somewhere outside, by candle-light.
Church bells ring out in the heat
And call to people in the street.
The Christmas story here is told
In summer, when the sun is gold.

JOAN MELLINGS

Christmas in Australia and New Zealand is especially exciting. School is over, the long summer holidays have started and Father Christmas has arrived in the city stores. He even comes up the river on water-skis in Surfers' Paradise! The decorated shops are crowded from morning until late at night.

Some families are already camping in tents and caravans at beach and river resorts. It is just the beginning of summer though so, while it is hot in some areas, people in the south may have quite a cool, wet Christmas.

Carol singing is held at night in many public parks. Everyone sits on the grass and sings by the light of twinkling candles. Thousands of people in Melbourne and Sydney attend 'Carols by Candlelight' on Christmas Eve, while many more watch it on TV and join in the singing at home.

The sun is up very early on Christmas Day and so is everyone else. Children discover that Father Christmas has been and presents are exchanged around the Christmas tree.

The churches are full of early worshippers, then everyone hurries home for dinner. Uncles, aunts, grandpas and grandmas are all there. Some even fly home from interstate or overseas. Even if the day is very hot, most people have a real celebration with bonbons, party hats, mountains of roast turkey, chicken or lamb, roast potatoes and other hot vegetables, followed by steaming plum pudding or a cold dessert — all washed down with plenty of cool drinks.

In the afternoon the children play with their new toys, splash in a backyard pool or visit the beach while the grown-ups sit and talk. Everyone always says they have eaten too much, but they still find room for a party tea of ham, salad, icecream and summer fruits. It is a day of togetherness for family and friends.

Tribal Aboriginal people get together for a feast of the

foods found in their area — kangaroo, turtle, fish or yabbies. The children receive gifts lovingly made by their parents: spear throwers, baby carriers, digging sticks — smaller models of the ones the adults use.

Even families who live on isolated cattle or sheep stations greet their distant neighbours on the radio in a 'galah session', after the Flying Doctor has given advice to his patients.

People from many different lands have made their homes in Australia and New Zealand. They have brought their own customs and recipes with them, but still the most popular way of celebrating Christmas is with a traditional 'English dinner'.

The next day, Boxing Day, is spent picnicking, attending a sporting event like the Test cricket, international tennis or the start of the Sydney-Hobart Yacht Race, or watching them quietly at home on TV.

Then the holidays start in earnest — camping, fishing, boating and swimming. After all that excitement, it is good to relax.

THE BEST CHRISTMAS PRESENT

'Out in the back country . . . the best Christmas present you could wish for is still to come — rain. You look out upon acre after acre of parched, brown land — but you swig a cold drink, tackle a healthy portion of cold meat, and know in your heart that as sure as it's His birthday, He won't let you down. It's been dry before, and it'll be dry again — but it's Christmas Day, so do not worry.'

CELEBRATION FOOD

On a special occasion, such as a birthday or a wedding, we often have celebration meals and eat special or traditional foods. At Christmas we are celebrating Jesus' birthday, and in many countries of the world people are very busy preparing special things to eat and drink. Often, the meal is eaten on Christmas Eve.

In **Denmark** dinner follows church at four o'clock. It is served on beautifully decorated tables. After dinner, everyone dances round the Christmas tree before opening presents.

In **Austria,** the family meal follows midnight service, as it does in **France** and **French Canada,** where the meal is called 'reveillon'.

Most people in **Britain,** and in countries that take their customs from the UK, eat traditional Christmas dinner around midday on Christmas Day itself.

FAVOURITE DISHES

Here are some favourite dishes — past and present — from different parts of the world:

Peacock was once served at rich tables in England. The skin and feathers were carefully pulled away while the bird was spit-roasted, then rearranged in all its glory. The beak was gilded before the bird was proudly borne to the table. It was probably very tough to eat!

Boar's head used to be a centre-piece. After being stuffed and cooked, the head was rubbed with lard mixed with soot, to give it a life-like colour. It was surrounded by a wreath of bay or rosemary.

Sucking pig, another favourite dish in England in the past, is served at Christmas in Cuba. It can be roasted on a spit or in the oven, basted frequently with butter and beer to make it crisp and brown.

Goose was served to Elizabeth I of England on 24 December as news came of the destruction of the Spanish

Armada. She decreed that goose should be eaten at Christmas ever after. The custom spread to Germany, where it is still the favourite choice, as it is in Denmark, where it is often cooked with a stuffing of prunes and apples.

Turkeys certainly don't come from Turkey, though some say they got their name from Turkish merchants who first imported the birds. The Spanish Conquistadors first discovered the birds in South America and introduced them to Europe. Henry VIII in England ate turkey on Christmas Day. But the USA has made turkey real celebration fare, eating it on Thanksgiving Day as well as Christmas. There is delicious cranberry sauce to go with it.

Christmas pie made from chicken, pork and veal is baked for *reveillon* in Canada.

Dried ling boiled up with white sauce flavoured with Jamaica pepper and black pepper is a traditional Swedish dish. The most typical dish is the big Christmas **ham,** eaten with mustard.

Bull's heart is served in Peru. It is quartered, marinaded in spice and wine vinegar, then spit-roasted over an open fire.

Sweet things are important at Christmas too. In many countries, batches of special biscuits are baked for the Christmas season. Most of them are spiced, like the German peppernuts, or *pfeffernusse,* or the dark molasses cookies that Moravian housewives, whose families settled in North Carolina, still bake in fancy shapes.

Christmas pudding has been eaten in England for many hundreds of years, but it began as a rich porridge, made from pieces of meat and dried fruits, thickened with brown breadcrumbs. As time went by the porridge became so thick that it was renamed pudding. Nowadays dried fruits, nuts, shredded suet, brown sugar, spices and breadcrumbs make the very special mixture, cooked many hours, that produces a dark rich Christmas pudding.

A different kind of pudding is served in Scandinavia. It is **rice porridge,** in which an almond has been hidden. The girl who finds the almond will be the next bride, so they say.

In France the traditional Christmas Eve sweet is a **Christmas log** It is rich, so you only need small helpings.

CHRISTMAS LOG TO MAKE

You need:
18 sweet biscuits
1 teaspoon cocoa powder
1 teaspoon icing sugar
1 small pot of double cream
extra icing sugar to decorate

Utensils: basin, whisk, fork, knife, teaspoon, plate, aluminium foil.

1
Put the cream, sugar and cocoa into a basin and whisk until the mixture is stiff enough to stand up in peaks.

2
Spread about half the quantity on to the biscuits, then sandwich the biscuits together to make a long roll.

3
Wrap the biscuit roll in foil and put it in the fridge. Put the rest of the cream mix in the fridge too.

4
Just before the meal, unwrap the roll and put it on a plate. Cover it with the rest of the cream, forking it lightly to look like tree bark. Sprinkle icing sugar on top and decorate with a sprig of plastic holly.

CHRISTMAS DAY

" *Dear God,*
I like Christmas because it's your birthday. Most
people like Christmas because of the presents. "
Dennis
From CHILDREN'S LETTERS TO GOD

At last Christmas Day — the birthday of Jesus — has arrived! Sometimes we feel that the day will never come, and perhaps it has always been that way. For hundreds of years before Jesus was born men and women were already waiting for the coming of a King and Saviour promised by God. The prophet Isaiah wrote many years before about the birth of a very special baby:

'A child is born to us!
A son is given to us!
And he will be our ruler.
He will be called "Wonderful Counsellor",
"Mighty God", "Eternal Father",
"Prince of Peace".
His royal power will continue to grow;
his kingdom will always be at peace.'

Mary had many months to wait after Gabriel, the angel, told her that she would be the mother of Jesus. But at last the time came. St Luke describes what happened.

THE BABY IS BORN

'At that time the Emperor Augustus ordered a census to be taken throughout the Roman Empire. When this first census took place, Quirinius was the governor of Syria. Everyone, then, went to register himself, each to his own town.

Joseph went from the town of Nazareth in Galilee to the town of Bethlehem in Judaea, the birthplace of King David. Joseph went there because he was a descendant of David. He went to register with Mary, who was promised in marriage to him. She was pregnant, and while they were in Bethlehem, the time came for her to have her baby. She gave birth to her first son, wrapped him in strips of cloth and laid him in a manger — there was no room for them to stay in the inn.'

'WORSHIP CHRIST, THE NEW-BORN KING'

All who saw the baby Jesus knelt down beside his crib and worshipped him. Angels, shepherds and wise men too knew that although he was so little and helpless, he was God's Son and King of the whole world. Christians everywhere worship Jesus on his birthday. To worship Jesus means to tell him how great and wonderful he is and to be full of happiness and praise to him. We can worship Jesus by keeping very quiet and still, as well as by singing carols with all our hearts and voices.

Sing aloud on this day!
Children all raise the lay.
Cheerfully we and they
Hasten to adore thee
Sent from highest glory.
For us born, born, born
For us born on this morn
Of the Virgin Mary.

All must join him to praise,
Men and boys voices raise
On this day of all days;
Angel voices ringing,
Christmas tidings bringing.
Join we all, all, all,
Join we all, 'Gloria
In excelsis' singing.

A 14th-CENTURY GERMAN CAROL, FIRST WRITTEN IN LATIN

What can I give him,
Poor as I am?
If I were a shepherd,
I would bring a lamb;
If I were a wise man,
I would do my part;
Yet what I can I give him —
Give my heart.

CHRISTINA ROSSETTI

PRESENTS FOR THE BABY

As well as worshipping and praising Jesus, we should like to give him a present on his birthday, just as the wise men did. The best birthday present we can give is our thankfulness and our love.

CHRISTMAS QUIZ

The Bible stories about Jesus' birth leave a lot to our imagination and from early times people have added to the bare facts given to us by St Matthew and St Luke. Nowadays, fact and tradition have become mixed. If you knew only what the Bible tells, what would be the answer to these questions?

★ What did Mary ride on the journey to Bethlehem?
★ How soon after they reached Bethlehem was Jesus born?
★ What was the weather like?
★ What sort of building was Jesus born in?
★ What part did the innkeeper play in the story?
★ What animals were gathered round the manger?
★ How many wise men were there?
★ How soon after Jesus' birth did they arrive?
★ How did they travel?

Read again the Christmas story in Matthew 2 and Luke 2: 1-20. You may get a surprise when you check your answers!

I Am a Donkey

by Sarah Tearle

One day When I was in my shed, Joseph brought me out and Mary climbed on my back. Then Joseph led the Way to bethlehem. When we Were there, there was No room in any of the inns So Joseph took us to a stable, in the night a baby Was born. Just then a sheep came in and said Out in the field I saw a bright light shaped like a person. It said to come here only Whats Special in a stable. I said Well, Look whats in my food box. That must be the special baby that the angel told us about, What's his name? Said the sheep, and I said His names Jesus, the sheep said Thats a nice name Why's he called Jesus? and I said When I was in my stable One day I saw a bright light like you saw and it said to Mary Soon you are going to have a baby you must call him Jesus because he is the Son of God. My Shepherd says it's time to go now, Good-bye. As soon as the sheep had Gone a camel came in and the camel said I followed a bright Star it was different from all the others and it led us here and I don't see Whats special in a stable. Well there's a baby in my food box called Jesus I said. He's a very special baby and I Love him very much. My master and my friends masters brought gifts for the baby said the camel. I think that they brought gold, frankincense and myrrh. I said those Sound nice presents for him.

THE SHEPHERDS

'There were some shepherds in that part of the country who were spending the night in the fields, taking care of their flocks. An angel of the Lord appeared to them, and the glory of the Lord shone over them. They were terribly afraid, but the angel said to them, "Don't be afraid! I am here with good news for you, which will bring great joy to all the people. This very day in David's town your Saviour was born — Christ the Lord! And this is what will prove it to you: you will find a baby wrapped in strips of cloth and lying in a manger."

Suddenly a great army of heaven's angels appeared with the angel, singing praises to God:

"Glory to God in the highest heaven, and peace on earth to those with whom he is pleased!"

When the angels went away from them back into heaven, the shepherds said to one another, "Let's go to Bethlehem and see this thing that has happened, which the Lord has told us."

So they hurried off and found Mary and Joseph and saw the baby lying in the manger. When the shepherds saw him, they told them what the angel had said about the child. All who heard it were amazed at what the shepherds said. Mary remembered all these things and thought deeply about them. The shepherds went back, singing praises to God for all they had heard and seen; it had been just as the angel had told them.'

LUKE'S GOSPEL, CHAPTER 2

Seth

by David Kossoff

About seventy. A weather-beaten, ruddy, lined face. A still, patient man. Bent, but still wiry and active-looking. Blue eyes, of a sharp intelligence, but kindly and interested. A deep countryman's voice.

My father and my grandfather were shepherds. It is a thing that runs in families. My sons own their own farms and their own sheep, but that is progress. I always looked after other people's sheep. Mind you, my sons are both clever, and quick in the mind, like my wife. She's always been rather a scholar. A good thing, for I can hardly read or write, but that was not unusual when I was younger. We were looked down on, I suppose, for often we had to work every day, ignoring the Sabbath, and with so many priests among the people, we were often told we were breaking the law. Though where the priests would have got their perfect lambs for sacrifice without us, I don't know. They could be very rude, the priests. Especially the young, silly ones. It's the same today. And not just with priests. People speak before they think. That's one good thing about looking after sheep. You get into the habit of keeping quiet. If you have to use words, you take your time to get them right. Words are important.

People often tell me that mine was a dull life. Well, maybe. Looking after sheep *is* much the same each day. But many people have never seen the lambs play and leap, have never sat quiet on a hill and watched the sun. Or the moon. I like to watch the night sky, the moon and the stars. Once I saw, at night, a sight that very few have seen. Just once, but once was enough for any man. If a priest is rude to me, I always say to myself, 'It doesn't matter, I had that night and you didn't.'

I was about nineteen at the time, and, although it's now about fifty years ago, I remember it like yesterday. I lived with my parents, not far from Jerusalem, and I was one of a group of shepherds who looked after the sheep owned by the Temple. As I said, the sheep for the Temple services have to be perfect, and a great many are bred for food, too. We, our group, usually worked at night. On this night I'm talking about, we'd met up where we usually did, on the side of quite a big hill. We'd had a bite to eat and drink and were sitting talking. Around us, our hundreds of sheep. All normal and usual and quiet. Very restful and pleasant, those talks at night. It was a dark night.

Then there was a sort of stillness and a feeling of change, of difference. We all felt it. I had a friend called Simon, and he first noticed what the change was. It was the light. There was a sort of paleness. It was a dark night but suddenly it wasn't dark. We began to see each other's faces very clearly in a sort of silvery shimmering light. We seemed surrounded and enclosed in a great glow. It was the purest light I ever saw. The sheep were white as snow. Then, as our eyes began to ache with it, just farther up the hill from us the glow seemed to intensify and take shape, and we saw a man. Like us but not like us. Taller, stiller. Though we were still enough, God knows.

He looked at us and we looked at him. We waited for him to speak. It didn't seem right (we all felt it) for any of us to speak first. He took his time — as though to find the right words — and then he began to tell us what he called good news of great joy. Of a new-born baby, born in David's town. A baby sent by God, to save the world, to change things, to make things better. He told us where to go and find the baby and how to recognize him. And to tell other people the good news. His own pleasure in telling us filled us with joy, too. We shared his pleasure — if you follow me. Then he stopped speaking and became two. Then four, then eight, and in a second there seemed to be a million like him. Right up the hill and on up into the sky. A

million. And they sang to us. 'Glory to God,' they sang, 'and on earth peace to all men.' It was wonderful. It came to an end and then they were gone. Every single one, and we felt lonely and lost.

Then Samuel, who was the eldest of us, said, 'Come, let us go and find the baby. David's town the angel said; Bethlehem. In a manger. In swaddling clothes.' And off we went. We ran, we sang, we shouted, we were important, we'd been chosen. We were special. We were on a search, we had to find a baby.

And we did find him. We were led there, There was no 'searching'. We were led, and we saw for ourselves. Not much to see, perhaps. A young mother and her husband and her newly born baby. Born in a stable because all the inns were full. Poor people they were. The man was a carpenter.

Well, we did as we'd been told, we spread the word, and people did get excited. But not for long. Nothing lasts. We shepherds were heroes for a while, but then everyone knew the story. It was old news. Soon we were just shepherds again. Doing a dull job. But we were different from all the rest. We'd had that night. I don't talk about it much any more. But it keeps me warm. I was there.

While shepherds kept their watching
O'er silent flocks by night,
Behold throughout the heavens
There shone a holy light.

CHORUS
Go tell it on the mountain,
Over the hills and everywhere,
Go tell it on the mountain
That Jesus Christ is born.

NORTH AMERICAN SPIRITUAL

WHEN THE ANIMALS SPEAK

Animals are not mentioned in the Bible stories about Christmas, but there are many Christmas legends about them. A twelfth-century carol describes how the donkey carried Mary to Bethlehem and the other animals looked after her and the new baby in the stable. The cow gave her manger for a bed and hay for a pillow and warmed the baby Jesus with her breath. The sheep gave her wool for a blanket and the doves cooed him to sleep.

On the first Christmas night the animals and birds were said to have talked about the wonderful news. People said they spoke in Latin, of course, because that was the language used in church. The words each spoke resembled the animal sounds they usually made. The cockerel crowed the good news — 'Christus natus est!' (Christ is born). The ox lowed 'Ubi?' (Where?) and the sheep bleated 'Bethlehem' in reply.

Every Christmas Eve since then, it was said, the cattle in their sheds fall on their knees on the stroke of midnight and talk in human language. The bees, too, gather in their hive and hum the Hundredth

Psalm. But never try to listen to any of them! It is said to be very unlucky!

ANIMALS FOR PRESENTS

Puppies, kittens and even horses, make exciting Christmas presents. But looking after an animal properly takes a great deal of time and money too. Food and veterinary care are expensive. Horses and dogs must be exercised and all pets need regular daily care and feeding, whether you feel like

bothering or not. New pets are sometimes turned out of the house after Christmas, once the owners find them too much trouble. Others are kept but are badly neglected. Before you ask to be given a pet, find out exactly what looking after it will involve. Remember that you are responsible to keep it happy and healthy for the rest of its life.

Don Pedro's Christmas

by Eric P. Keely

adapted by Mala Powers

Madre Marta was firm in declaring that Don Pedro could not go to the Christmas Eve service with Lolla.

'But Don Pedro is so good,' begged Lolla. 'He works all the time. I would just tie him up outside the church door. I know he would be quiet.'

'All right,' sighed Lolla's mother, finally agreeing 'take him along if you wish.'

Lolla's face was radiant as she ran out from the small square adobe dwelling in the New Mexican valley where they lived, and hurried to her pet.

'My good little burro,' she exclaimed, throwing her arms round the donkey's neck, 'I just couldn't go to church without you.' Lolla was lucky that she could express her love to Don Pedro in words, while he could only twitch his ears to show his affection.

The weather had been very warm and, on this particular day before Christmas, it was unusually hot. 'If the heat spell goes on,' Lolla's father said, 'too much snow will melt in the hills and the river could overflow!'

As darkness came, the family prepared to go to the church; and Lolla went to get Don Pedro, but the little donkey was not in his shed.

'Don Pedro has wandered off,' Lolla called to her mother. 'I will find him and meet you at the church.'

She took a lantern and began her search. It wasn't far from the adobe house to the church — just down the road, over the river's bridge, and up to the small steepled chapel. As Lolla searched for Don Pedro, she saw the people of the valley walking or driving their cars to the midnight service.

After looking everywhere for Don Pedro, without success, Lolla started walking towards the church. As she crossed the old bridge she felt it sway more than usual. The water in the river was very high. How black it was, how swift! Suddenly Lolla's heart began to pound. Something was moving near the river's edge.

'Who's there?' she called out. In response came the loud raucous braying of a donkey.

'Don Pedro!' Lolla gasped and, sliding down the bank to the water's edge, she found her

54

little burro! There he was, stuck in the mud and water by the bridge.

Lolla set down her lantern and, quickly wading out into the rising river, she stretched out her arms and seized her pet's tail in both hands.

'Kick, Don Pedro,' she commanded, 'kick as hard as you can!'

Don Pedro obeyed as Lolla tugged with all her might, and at last the little burro kicked himself free of the mud and came charging out of the water.

As Lolla picked up the lantern, its light disclosed something that made her gasp.

'Don Pedro,' she cried, flinging herself upon the little donkey's back, 'go quickly. Go as fast as you can!'

Inside the old church good Padre Carlos had just finished telling of the joys and blessings of Christmas. Suddenly the door of the church swung wide, and up the aisle came, of all things, a little burro, soggy and wet and covered with mud.

'What sacrilege is this?' cried the padre.

'Such a disturbance in a church!' Then he saw the small girl, almost as wet and muddy as the donkey.

'Oh Padre,' Lolla cried, 'I'm so glad we got here in time. The bridge is all washed out at the bottom. If anyone drives over it in a car it will fall. People will be killed.' The whole congregation rose to its feet in alarm as Lolla blurted out her story.

When she finished, Padre Carlos touched the little donkey with tender hands.

'God works in mysterious ways,' he said. 'Let us give thanks that perhaps lives have been saved through Lolla and this little burro.'

Lolla glanced at Don Pedro quietly standing beside her. As she lovingly scratched the fuzzy head, she remembered another little donkey who had stood by the baby Jesus in a stable 2,000 years earlier.

'Yes,' she thought, 'Don Pedro has a right to be here in church on this Christmas Eve.'

REMEMBER THE BIRDS

Many Christmas legends have to do with birds. The cockerel in the stable yard at Bethlehem was said to be the first creature to proclaim Christ's birth, crowing just that once at midnight instead of dawn. 'Christus natus est!' (Christ is born). That is why midnight mass on Christmas Eve is called the Mass of the Rooster in Spanish and Latin American countries.

In Scandinavia people remember the birds by hanging out a sheaf of corn or other food birds like, fastened to a pole, on their snow-covered gardens on Christmas Eve. If you live in a country where Christmas comes at the cold time of year, you might like to make a bird 'bell'.

BIRD BELL

You will need:
225g/1 cup fat
unsalted peanuts
raisins and breadcrumbs

Utensils: empty margarine tub (or half coconut shell which the birds have pecked clean), saucepan, spoon, string, metal skewer or nail.

1
Make four small holes near the rim of the tub, at equal distances, using a skewer or nail.*

2
Melt the fat in pan over a very low heat (NB hot fat can burn badly).*

3
When the fat has melted stir in breadcrumbs, raisins and peanuts and leave mixture to cool.

4
When cool, pour into tub or shell and leave to harden completely. If you push a stick into the centre of the mixture before it hardens it will make a perch for the birds to cling to.

5
Tie the tub securely, threading string through holes in both directions to join at top. Leave enough string to tie tub upside down on tree or garden post. (NB hang well away from cats and your mother's washing line!)

Don't expect the birds to come and feed at once, it may be several days before they pluck up courage to investigate anything new.

Ask a grown-up to help with this.

A Gift for Gramps

by Aileen Fisher
adapted by Mala Powers

'What are you going to give Gramps for Christmas?' Louella asked her brother as she stared at her Christmas list.

'That's just what I was going to ask you,' replied Johnny. 'I'm stumped.' The two children were sitting alone at the kitchen table. Their half-finished Christmas lists lay before them.

'Gramps always gets socks and handkerchiefs — handkerchiefs and socks,' continued Johnny. 'He has enough to last another hundred years!'

'I know,' said Louella. 'And we can't get him sports things because with his legs so full of rheumatism, poor Gramps just sits in his chair by the window. I wish we could think of something that would be fun for him every day to help him forget his pain.'

So they thought and they thought. Louella closed her eyes, and Johnny stared out of the window at the snowy yard. As he watched, a quick little bird flew to the window-sill, looked into the room, and then flew away.

Suddenly Johnny jumped up from his chair in great excitement. 'I've got it!' he shouted.

'Got what?' asked Louella.

'Why, the present for Gramps. It's perfect, and the whole family could be in on it!'

On Christmas morning, when Gramps had hobbled to his favourite chair by the window, Johnny said, 'Gramps, we wanted to give you something different this year. Something that would be fun for a long time. Now turn around, and look out of the window!'

Gramps turned to look. There, attached to the sill, was a wide new shelf with a moulding around its edge. And on the shelf were all sorts of things that birds like to eat: seeds and suet and dabs of peanut butter and bits of dry bread.

'I made the feeding-station,' Johnny explained. 'And Louella got the supply of bird food for you, Gramps.' Johnny held his breath as he saw a snowbird perch on the edge of the feeding-station and then fearlessly peck at some seeds.

'Well, I'll be . . .' Gramps said. 'Look at that!'

Then, with a red and grey flash of wings, another bird swooped down.

'What in the world kind of bird is that?' asked Gramps.

'Ah,' said mother, 'that's where my present comes in.' She reached under the boughs of the Christmas tree and pulled out a package which was hidden there. 'Merry Christmas, Grandpa!'

Gramps opened the package excitedly. There before him was a big book with beautiful coloured pictures of hundreds of birds.

'Well, this is something!' Gramps exclaimed, turning the pages. 'I never knew there were so many birds.'

Sometime later, Gramps gave a shout. 'A pine grosbeak! That's what that red and grey bird was: a pine grosbeak!' He grinned with pleasure at being such a good detective. He had forgotten all about his aching rheumatism!

'This is the best Christmas present I ever got,' Gramps said.

Of course, Johnny and Louella received Christmas presents that Christmas too; but what they always remembered best was the gift of giving from their hearts — a gift for Gramps.

THE CHRISTMAS CRIB

> *This is the day which the Lord hath made: let us rejoice and be glad in it.*
> *For the beloved and most holy Child had been given to us and born for us by the wayside*
> *And hid in a manger because he had no room in the inn.*
> *Glory to God in the highest: and on earth peace to men of good will.*
>
> *From ST FRANCIS' VESPERS FOR CHRISTMAS*

It was Christmas Eve 1223 at Greccio, not far from Francis' home town of Assisi. Clattering feet rang on the stony path up the mountain side and voices hummed excitedly. Then the footsteps and voices stopped abruptly. Torches and candles lit up the entrance to a cave in the mountain. Within the flickering shadows of the cave the watchers could make out the gently breathing forms of an ox and a donkey, standing patiently beside the carved wooden figure of a baby in a crib.

As the villagers watched, St Francis began to tell the story of the first Christmas, taking the part of each character in turn. For too long the incarnation had been a subject to be studied by learned theologians and priests. Francis was determined that ordinary men and women should understand what it meant for God's Son to be born in a poor and dirty stable.

St Francis' Christmas crib became a special occasion every Christmas. Soon he provided a real baby instead of the carved wooden one he had ordered the first year. He always chose an orphan with no home, because he knew that afterwards the child would be well cared for.

In the centuries that followed, Francis' idea of a Christmas crib spread all over Europe. They were set up in churches and later in homes, where still today in some countries they are the centre of the Christmas worship.

NAMES FOR THE CHRISTMAS CRIB AROUND THE WORLD

Presipio —	Italy
Crèche —	France
Krippe —	Germany
Naciemiento —	Spain, Guatemala and other Latin American countries
Jeslicky —	Czechoslovakia
Pesebre —	Brazil
Portal —	Costa Rica

In Marseilles a special fair is held in December when small terra cotta figures are sold to be used in crib scenes. As well as representing the holy family, there are figures of the local butcher, baker, policeman and priest.

CRADLE ROCKING

About two hundred years after Francis, in the fifteenth century, it became the custom to hold a special Christmas Eve service round the crib in the churches in Germany. The priests, acting as Joseph and Mary, would rock the cradle. Then all the congregation would join in, dancing and singing carols and rocking the cradle as they passed. Here is a verse from an old German rocking carol:

And who would rock the cradle
Wherein this infant lies,
Must rock with easy motion
And watch with humble eyes,
Like Mary pure and wise.

A MODERN ST FRANCIS

A clergyman working in Birmingham decided that the ready-made plastic nativity scenes on sale in the shops round his church, gave a false impression of the first Christmas. This is what he did.

'I got together with a group of boys and we built a life-sized stable in the back of the church, built it out of wood from old houses that were being demolished . . . And we borrowed two tailors' dummies and dressed them in genuine Palestinian costume. When we came to arrange them, one of the boys said, "We'll have Mary lying down, like my mum is when she's had a baby." So Mary lay down on a cloak in the straw while Joseph slumped up against a pillar, like most expectant fathers after the event.

'What we were trying to do was to introduce some reality and we thought we might have succeeded when two people came out of the stable and one said, "Oh, wasn't that nice?" and the other said, "No. No," he said, "it was a lousy, horrible place to be born."

'Last week over ten thousand people went through the stable in that church.'

The Story of Baboushka

retold by Arthur Scholey

All the villagers were out, bubbling with excitement.

'Did you see it again last night?'

'Of course we did.'

'Much bigger.'

'It was moving, coming towards us. Tonight it will be high above us.'

That night, excitement, like a wind, scurried through the lanes and alleys.

'There's been a message.'

'An army is on the way.'

'Not an army — a procession.'

'Horses and camels and treasure.'

Now everyone was itching for news. No one could work. No one could stay indoors.

No one, that is, but Baboushka. Baboushka had work to do — she always had. She swept, polished, scoured and shined. Her house was the best kept, best polished, best washed and painted. Her garden was beautiful, her cooking superb.

'All this fuss for a star!' she muttered. 'I haven't time even to look. I'm so behind, I must work all night!'

So, she missed the star at its most dazzling, high overhead. She missed the line of twinkling lights coming towards the village at dawn. She missed the sound of pipes and drums, the tinkling of bells getting louder. She missed the voices and whispers and then the sudden quiet of the villagers, and the footsteps coming up the path to her door. But the knocking! She couldn't miss that.

'Now what?' she demanded, opening the door. Baboushka gaped in astonishment. There were three kings at her door! And a servant.

'My masters seek a place to rest,' he said. 'Yours is the best house in the village.'

'You . . . want to stay here?'

'It would only be till night falls and the star appears again.'

Baboushka gulped. 'Come in, then,' she said.

How the kings' eyes sparkled at the sight of the home-baked bread, the meat pies, the cakes, jams and pickles.

As she dashed about, serving them, Baboushka asked question after question.

'Have you come a long way?'

'Very far,' sighed Caspar.

'And where are you going?'

'We're following the star,' said Melchior.

'But where?'

They didn't know, they told her. But they believed that it would lead them, in the end, to a new-born king, a king such as the world had never seen before, a king of Earth and Heaven.

'Why don't you come with us?' said Balthasar. 'Bring him a gift as we do. See, I bring gold, and my colleagues bring spices and ointments.'

'Oh,' said Baboushka, 'I am not sure that he

60

would welcome me. And as for a gift . . .'

'This excellent pickle's fit for any king!' cried Balthasar.

Baboushka laughed. 'Pickle? For a baby? A baby needs toys.' She paused. 'I have a cupboard full of toys,' she said sadly. 'My baby son, my little king, died while very small.'

Balthasar stopped her as she bustled once more to the kitchen.

'This new king could be your king, too. Come with us when the star appears tonight,' he said.

'I'll . . . I'll think about it,' sighed Baboushka.

As the kings slept, Baboushka cleaned and tidied as quietly as she could. What a lot of extra work there was! And this new king. What a funny idea — to go off with the kings to find him. Yet, could she possibly do it, leave home and go looking for him just like that?

Baboushka shook herself. No time for dreaming! All this washing-up, and putting away of dishes, and extra cooking. Anyway, how long would she be away? What would she wear? And what about gifts?

She sighed. 'There is so much to do. The house will have to be cleaned when they've gone. I couldn't just leave it.'

Suddenly it was night-time again. There was the star!

'Are you ready, Baboushka?'

'I'll . . . I'll come tomorrow,' Baboushka called. 'I'll catch up. I must just tidy here, find a gift, get ready . . .'

The kings waved sadly. The star shone ahead. Baboushka ran back into the house, eager to get on with her work.

Sweeping, dusting, beating all the cushions and carpets, cleaning out the kitchen, cooking — away went the night.

At last she went to the small cupboard, opened the door and gazed sadly once again at all those toys. But goodness me, how dusty they were! One thing was certain. They weren't fit for a baby king. They would all need to be

cleaned. Better get started at once.

On, on she worked. One by one the toys glowed, glistened and gleamed. There! Now they would be fit for the royal baby.

Baboushka looked through the window. It was dawn! Clear on the air came the sound of the farm cockerel. She looked up. The star had gone. The kings would have found somewhere else to rest by now. She would easily catch them up.

At the moment, though, she felt so tired. Surely she could rest now — just for an hour.

Suddenly, she was wide awake. It was dark. She had slept all day! She ran out into the street. No star. She rushed back into the house, pulled on her cloak, hurriedly packed the toys in a basket and stumbled down the path the kings had taken.

On she went, hurrying through village after village. Everywhere she asked after the kings.

'Oh yes,' they told her, 'we saw them. They went that way.'

Days passed and Baboushka lost count. The villages grew bigger and became towns. But Baboushka never stopped, through night and day. Then she came to a city. The palace! she thought. That's where the royal baby would be born.

'No royal baby here,' said the palace guard.

'Three kings? What about them?' asked Baboushka.

'Ah yes, they came, But they didn't stay long. They were soon on their journey.'

'But where to?'

'Bethlehem, that was the place. I can't imagine why. It's a very poor place. But that's where they went.'

She set off at once.

It was evening when Babousnka wearily arrived at Bethlehem. How many days had she been on the journey? She could not remember. And could this really be the place for a royal baby? It didn't look like it. It was not much bigger than her own village. She went to the inn.

'Oh yes,' said the landlord, 'the kings were here two days ago. There was great excitement. But they didn't even stay the night.'

'And a baby?' Baboushka cried. 'Was there a baby?'

'Yes,' said the landlord, 'there was. Those kings asked to see the baby, too.'

When he saw the disappointment in Baboushka's eyes, he stopped.

'If you'd like to see where the baby was,' he said quickly, 'it was across the yard there. I couldn't offer the couple anything better at the time. My inn was packed full. They had to go in the stable.'

Baboushka followed him across the yard.

'Here's the stable,' he said. Then he left her.

'Baboushka?'

Someone was standing in the half-light of the doorway. He looked kindly at her. Perhaps he knew where the family had gone? She knew now that the baby king was the most important thing in the world to her.

'They have gone to Egypt, and safety,' he told Baboushka. 'And the kings have returned to their kingdoms another way. But one of them told me about you. I am sorry but, as you see, you are too late. Shepherds came as soon as the angels told them. The kings came as soon as they saw the star. It was Jesus the Christ-child they found, the world's Saviour.'

It is said that Baboushka is still looking for the Christ-child, for time means nothing in the search for things that are real. Year after year she goes from house to house calling, 'Is he here? Is the Christ-child here?'

Particularly at Christmas, when she sees a sleeping child and hears of good deeds, she will lift out a toy from her basket and leave it, just in case.

Then, on she goes with her journey, still searching, still calling, 'Is he here? Is the Christ-child here?'

CHRISTMAS IN PRISON

> **"** *Remember those who are in prison, as though you were in prison with them. Remember those who are suffering, as though you were suffering as* **"** *they are.*
> HEBREWS 13:3

...many
...from home
...ed in prisons
...ome will be
...y have
...f the land,
...urage in
...es in a
...ds religious
...xpect them
... Christmas,
...d memories
...pression.

___

...STMASSY'

...from
...gland, was
...ailand on a
...harge. While
...e became a

Christian, and despair gave way to hope. In a radio interview she recalled Christmas in jail.

'I had only been a Christian for about three weeks. I had been given a song book with carols in it and I remember I took it and put it on my sewing machine in the workroom. There was so much noise coming from the machines and the Thai music being played, that no one heard me as I sang the carols, noticing the words for the first time. Christmas had been stripped bare of all the trimmings — the usual things like parties and presents — but somehow it made the real meaning come through more clearly. It was Christmassy in that real sense.'

1943 — '
IN A VER

Dietrich Bor
theologian a
to death in a
after being i
anti-fascist b

November
'If I should s
Christmas, o
me. I shoul
frightened a
can keep Cl
prison . . .'

December
'For a Chris
nothing pec
about Chris
cell. I daresa

meaning and will be observed with greater sincerity here in this prison than in places where all that survives of the feast is its name. That misery, suffering, poverty, loneliness, helplessness and guilt look very different to the eyes of God from what they do to man, that God should come down to the very place which men usually abhor, that Christ was born in a stable because there was no room for him in the inn — these are things which a prisoner can understand better than anyone else. For him the Christmas story is glad tidings in a very real sense . . .

'On Christmas Eve I shall be thinking of you all very much and I want you to believe that I too shall have a few hours of real joy and that I am not allowing my troubles to get the better of me.'
From LETTERS AND PAPERS FROM PRISON

1981 —
CHRISTMAS JOY

Strict Regime labor camp AK-159/40, Dolinka, Kazakhstan, Christmas 1981
'A Soviet prison camp would not be one's first choice of a place to spend Christmas. Rudolf Klassen and Vanya Pauls didn't exactly choose to be there either. Rudolf Klassen was half-way through a three-year sentence for youth work in the unregistered Baptist church here in Karaganda; Vanya Pauls, from the Baptist church in nearby Shaktinsk, had recently been sentenced

to four years' imprisonment . . .
'Vanya arrived in the camp on December 10, and was immediately asked by the camp authorities to promise not to preach; when he refused he was promptly punished by 15 days in the isolation cell. Christmas Day brought release, reunion with Rudolf Klassen and the opportunity to write home:

Christmas Eve in the Cells
'Although here I had no chance to be with you physically, I prayed and rejoiced with tears in my eyes yesterday evening . . .
'How great is the world, yet even greater is the joy of Christmas embracing the hearts of all who are saved. Although that evening I had only a mug of hot water and a hunk of gray bread, my joy often overflowed my heart and tears washed my cheeks. What rivers of joy and tears for you in your prayers, during your services . . .'

On *New Year's Eve* Rudolf Klassen wrote:
'I don't complain at my fate, no, I thank the Lord for this path. There is a saying: "You won't know happiness until you have experienced the bitterness of misfortune." And I must say that I have had to taste this in order to see happiness as a blessing from God . . .
'I remember, I once heard of a Christian prisoner, who drew a cross, and above it he wrote "height", below "depth" and on each side "length" and "breadth"; on the cross he

wrote: "love." It makes sense: . . . the cross of Christ unites us, and not just in some vague way, for we experience inexpressible bliss.'
From KESTON COLLEGE NEWS LETTER

THE PEACE-MAKER

Long before Jesus was born Isaiah said: 'A child is born to us! A son is given to us! . . . He will be called . . . "Prince of peace." '

Micah said: 'He will bring peace.'

At his birth the angels sang: 'Glory to God in the highest heaven and peace on earth.'

THE PEACE-CHILD

Don and Carol Richardson left Canada for New Guinea to tell the good news about Jesus Christ to the tribes living there. There was constant mistrust and treachery between neighbouring tribes and fighting constantly broke out. But the tribespeople had found

one way to keep peace. Each chief would hand over a child of his own tribe into the care of the enemy. Provided the adopted child was healthy and alive, there would be no war. If the child died, fighting broke out once more. For that reason the 'peace-child' was looked after carefully and well.

Don used this custom as a

way of explaining the coming of Jesus. God had given his own, much-loved Son as a peace-child to mankind, to show that he wants to be friends with us. But unlike the tribes' peace-child, this bringer of peace with God can never die. So when men and women accept God's peace-child, they know that never again need there be war between them and God.

Many of the listening Sawi people understood that message and became Christians. Love took the place of fear and hatred and soon they wanted to spread that love to their one-time enemies, the tribe living nearest to them.

It was Christmas time. They sent an invitation to come across in their canoes on a visit. The Sawis spread a splendid feast and when their neighbours arrived, with some trepidation, they were welcomed with carols and gifts of food.

After the feasting a Sawi read the verse from Isaiah which says, 'Unto us a child is born, to us a son is given.'

One look at the changed faces and manners of their old enemies was enough to assure the visitors that the story of the peace-child from heaven was real. It had changed their enemies into friends.

'WHY DO WE FIGHT?'

In December 1914 German and British forces stood facing each other, separated by a strip of flat ugly land intersected with barbed wire. Now and then shadowy figures crept across the waste of 'no-man's land,' but most of the soldiers kept well down below the skyline, enduring the mud and water that seeped into the trenches, intent only on avoiding firing from enemy lines opposite.

On Christmas Eve the air was cold and frost-filled. Suddenly, amazed British soldiers saw lights come on along the line of enemy trenches. Then came the unbelievable sound of singing — German soldiers singing 'Silent Night, Holy Night'. When the sound died away the British soldiers replied with 'The First Nowell'.

The singing by both sides went on for an hour and was followed by invitations to cross over to enemy lines. One German with great courage began to walk across to the British trenches, followed by other Germans, hands in pockets, to show that they had no weapons.

'I am a Saxon, you are Anglo-saxons. Why do we fight?' he asked.

When Christmas Day dawned bright and cold there was no sound of rifles or gunfire. The men had agreed among themselves to declare peace.

'A spirit stronger than war was at work that night,' one onlooker commented.

The top commanders of both sides did not approve. They knew that friendship between declared enemies would hinder warfare. But the truce continued. Even the wild birds, who had long ago forsaken the noisy battlefield, returned and were fed by the soldiers.

If the men had been free to obey their own wish for friendship and peace and the truce had not ended when Christmas was over, the lives of nearly nine million men would have been saved. That was the number who died before the armistice of November 1918.

One British soldier who took part in that memorable Christmas peace died in 1981 at the age of 85. To the end of his life he could not hear the singing of Silent Night without the tears streaming down his face. He remembered the German friends he made that Christmas who, for all he knew, he killed in the days that followed.

Christmas at the Little House in the Big Woods

by Laura Ingalls Wilder

Aunt Eliza and Uncle Peter and the cousins, Peter and Alice and Ella, were coming to spend Christmas.

The day before Christmas they came. Laura and Mary heard the gay ringing of sleigh bells, growing louder every moment, and then the big bobsled came out of the woods and drove up to the gate. Aunt Eliza and Uncle Peter and the cousins were in it, all covered up, under blankets and robes and buffalo skins.

They were wrapped up in so many coats and mufflers and veils and shawls that they looked like big, shapeless bundles.

When they all came in, the little house was full and running over. Black Susan ran out and hid in the barn, but Jack leaped in circles through the snow, barking as though he would never stop. Now there were cousins to play with! . . .

They played so hard all day that when night came they were too excited to sleep. But they must sleep, or Santa Claus would not come. So they hung their stockings by the fireplace, and said their prayers, and went to bed — Alice and Ella and Mary and Laura all in one bed on the floor.

Peter had the trundle bed, Aunt Eliza and Uncle Peter were going to sleep in the big bed, and another bed was made on the attic floor for Pa and Ma. The buffalo robes and all the blankets had been brought in from Uncle Peter's sled, so there were enough covers for everybody . . .

In the morning they all woke up almost at the same moment. They looked at their stockings, and something was in them. Santa Claus had been there. Alice and Ella and Laura in their red flannel nightgowns and Peter in his red flannel nightshirt, all ran shouting to see what he had brought.

In each stocking there was a pair of bright red mittens and there was a long flat stick of red-and-white-striped, pepper-mint candy, all beautifully notched along each side.

They were all so happy they could hardly speak at first. They just looked with shining eyes at those lovely Christmas presents. But Laura was happiest of all. Laura had a rag doll.

She was a beautiful doll. She had a face of white cloth with black button eyes. A black pencil had made her eyebrows, and her cheeks and her mouth were red with the ink made from pokeberries. Her hair was black yarn that had been knit and ravelled, so that it was curly.

She had little red flannel stockings and little black cloth gaiters for shoes, and her dress was pretty pink and blue calico.

She was so beautiful that Laura could not say a word. She just held her tight and forgot everything else. She did not know that everyone was looking at her, till Aunt Eliza said:

'Did you ever see such big eyes!'

The other girls were not jealous because Laura had mittens, and candy, *and* a doll, because Laura was the littlest girl, except Baby Carrie and Aunt Eliza's little baby, Dolly Varden. The babies were too small for dolls. They were so small they did not even know about Santa Claus. They just put their fingers in their mouths and wriggled because of all the excitement.

Laura sat down on the edge of the bed and held her doll. She loved her red mittens and she loved the candy, but she loved her doll best of all. She named her Charlotte.

Then they all looked at each other's mittens, and tried on their own, and Peter bit a large piece out of his stick of candy, but Alice and Ella and Mary and Laura licked theirs, to make it last longer . . .

Ma said, 'Laura, aren't you going to let the other girls hold your doll?' She meant, 'Little girls must not be so selfish.'

So Laura let Mary take the beautiful doll, and then Alice held her a minute, and then Ella. They smoothed the pretty dress and admired the red flannel stockings and the gaiters, and the curly woollen hair. But Laura was glad when at last Charlotte was safe in her arms again.

Pa and Uncle Peter had each a pair of new, warm mittens, knit in little squares of red and white. Ma and Aunt Eliza had made them.

Aunt Eliza had brought Ma a large red apple stuck full of cloves. How good it smelled! And it would not spoil, for so many cloves would keep it sound and sweet.

Ma gave Aunt Eliza a little needle-book she had made, with bits of silk for covers and soft white flannel leaves into which to stick the needles. The flannel would keep the needles from rusting.

They all admired Ma's beautiful bracket, and Aunt Eliza said that Uncle Peter had made one for her — of course, with different carving.

Santa Claus had not given them anything at all. Santa Claus did not give grown people presents, but that was not because they had not been good. Pa and Ma were good. It was because they were grown up, and grown people must give each other presents . . .

Today the weather was so cold that they could not play outdoors, but there were the new mittens to admire, and the candy to lick. And they all sat on the floor together and looked at the pictures in the Bible, and the pictures of all kinds of animals and birds in Pa's big green book. Laura kept Charlotte in her arms the whole time.

Then there was the Christmas dinner. Alice and Ella and Peter and Mary and Laura did not say a word at table, for they knew that children should be seen and not heard. But they did not need to ask for second helpings. Ma and Aunt Eliza kept their plates full and let them eat all the good things they could hold.

'Christmas comes but once a year,' said Aunt Eliza.

Dinner was early, because Aunt Eliza, Uncle Peter, and the cousins had such a long way to go.

'Best the horses can do,' Uncle Peter said, 'we'll hardly make it home before dark.'

So as soon as they had eaten dinner, Uncle Peter and Pa went to put the horses to the sled, while Ma and Aunt Eliza wrapped up the cousins.

They pulled heavy woollen stockings over the woollen stockings and the shoes they were already wearing. They put on mittens and coats and warm hoods and shawls, and wrapped mufflers around their necks and thick woollen veils over their faces. Ma slipped piping hot baked potatoes into their pockets to keep their fingers warm, and Aunt Eliza's flat-irons were hot on the stove, ready to put at their feet in the sled. The blankets and the quilts and the buffalo robes were warmed, too.

So they all got into the big bobsled, cosy and warm, and Pa tucked the last robe well in around them.

'Good-bye! Good-bye!' they called, and off they went, the horses trotting gaily and the sleigh bells ringing.

In just a little while the merry sound of the bells was gone, and Christmas was over. But what a happy Christmas it had been!

TRAVELLERS

Outside the warmth and light of church or home it is very dark. There may be travellers out there. Joseph and Mary, themselves, must have travelled with great weariness at night. So, in Ireland, a candle is lighted and put in the window to guide any such wanderers. The table too may be set with bread and milk and the door left unlatched, in case Mary and Joseph want to come in and rest.

In the days of the czars in Russia, peasants who lived in Siberia would put a portion of the Christmas feast just inside a darkened window for those 'whom nobody must see'. They were helping prisoners, escaping from the frozen bitter wastes of that desolate land, who could travel safely only by night.

The Kings

Three kings from Persian lands afar
To Jordan follow the pointing star:
And this is the quest of the travellers three,
Where the new born king of the Jews may be
Full royal gifts they bear for the King;
Gold, incense, myrrh are their offering.

The star shines out with a steadfast ray;
The kings to Bethlehem make their way,
And there in worship they bend the knee,
As Mary's child in her lap they see;
Their royal gifts they bear for the king;
Gold, incense, myrrh are their offering.

Thou child of man — lo, to Bethlehem
The kings are travelling — travel with them!
The star of mercy, the star of grace,
Shall lead thy heart to its resting place.
Gold, incense, myrrh thou canst not bring;
Offer thy heart to the infant King,
Offer thy heart!

Journey of a Lifetime

by David Kossoff

While Mary and Joseph were in Bethlehem others, far away, had begun a journey to find the Christ. David Kossoff tells the imaginary story of one member of that band of travellers.

I never liked to travel much. One of my brothers was a merchant and he travelled all his life. It was his livelihood, his work. He had no choice. I think perhaps this place, where I was born and have always lived, has something to do with my dislike of travelling. Babylon, on the mighty Euphrates, has everything a man needs. I had no need of travel. But once, only once, I went on a remarkable journey. A long journey, a search.

It is a long time ago, but I remember it as clear as if it were yesterday. I was about thirty at the time, and I lived and worked in the home of a man nearly twice my age. I was a scribe, and had a certain skill with figures. My master was a scholar and astrologer. He had spent his life in the study of planets and stars. It was part of his religion, of mine, too. He was famous. His family was old and among his forebears had been soothsayers to the Persian court, lawmakers to the Medes, men of prophecy and divination. He was a silent, large man — with deep-sunk eyes. Often he would not speak for days and then would dictate to me, or just talk, as though to think out loud; to sort the mind.

For about three years, he had been studying

Well, one day my master seemed rather excited. A friend of his from a place up north on the Tigris had been staying with us, and they had been deep in study and discussion for days. And up most of the night studying the stars.

'Something is happening,' said my master, 'something big. A whole series of signs and prophecies seem to be forming a pattern. We have been working separately and apart — and our conclusions agree. In two days' time we will have a third opinion. Have a room prepared.'

And in two days a third friend arrived. I knew him well. A big, friendly man. I met him at the gate.

'Hallo,' he said, 'where are they? There's something big going on. Don't unpack my bags, pack theirs. We have to stop looking at stars, we have to start following one!'

We started the very next night. There was a lot to arrange but the three of them were energetic and lively as schoolboys. They pointed out the star.

'A new one,' they said, with wonder, 'and it moves and gets brighter and we have found words and prophecies. We have to go and find a king and speak to him of another king greater than he, and we have to take for the greater king worthy presents. As the Queen of Sheba long ago took gifts to King Solomon, so we, too, have to go to Israel with gifts for a king!'

the Scriptures and the religion of the Jews of Israel, far to the west. He admired them.

'A remarkable people,' he would say, 'with a remarkable history, all written down. A history full of prophets and prophecies. A people who seem to be waiting. For a Savior, a leader, a Messiah.'

My master was in close touch with other scholars and astrologers like himself. He and they were of the tribe called magi, or wise men. Philosophers, thinkers, men of influence. Teachers, they were, and priests.

75

FOLLOW THE STAR

O star of wonder, star of night,
Star with royal beauty bright,
Westward leading, still proceeding,
Guide us to thy perfect light.

JOHN HENRY HOPKINS

'**J**esus was born in the town of Bethlehem in Judaea, during the time when Herod was king. Soon afterwards, some men who studied the stars came from the east to Jerusalem and asked, "Where is the baby born to be the king of the Jews? We saw his star when it came up in the east, and we have come to worship him." '

From MATTHEW'S GOSPEL, CHAPTER 2

WHAT WAS THE STAR?

Down the centuries, astronomers, who study stars, as well as ordinary people, have puzzled over which star it was that the wise men saw. Around the time that Jesus was born, the planets Saturn and Jupiter were unusually close, which would have made the sky specially bright. At about that time, too, Halley's comet would have been visible, shooting across the night sky. But none of the suggestions that has been made quite fits the case.

Certainly the wise men recognized the star as a sign of the birth of a king.

Hundreds of years before, a non-Jewish prophet had said,
'I look into the future,
And I see the nation of Israel.
A king, like a bright star, will arise in that nation.
Like a comet he will come from Israel.'
BIBLE BOOK OF NUMBERS 24 : 17

Perhaps the magi had heard that saying. They were sure enough to set off on a long journey to find the new king.

WIGILIA IN POLAND

When evening comes on Christmas Eve in Poland, everyone is very hungry. The day has been kept as a fast and now supper has to wait until the first star appears in the night sky. Just as the wise men gazed anxiously up to see their star, so the children peer upwards, each hoping to be the first to see a star twinkling in the cold night sky. At last someone calls out, 'Look! A star!' The greetings are exchanged and the special supper begins.

Once supper is over, the **Star Man** arrives. **Star boys,** dressed in all kinds of fancy costume, often come with him. First the Star Man makes sure that the children know their catechism, then he rewards them with small presents. After the Star boys have sung carols and everyone has enjoyed the fun, all set off to the midnight service in church.

Star boys are out and about again on 6 January, the date that marks the visit of the wise men to Jesus.

In Norway as well as Poland, boys dress up as the wise men as well as other characters in the Christmas story. They go from house to house singing carols and hoping for some treats in return. They carry paper stars on poles with candles inside the stars to make them shine.

CHRISTMAS STARS TO MAKE

Here are two kinds of Christmas star to make. You can put one large one on top of the Christmas tree, or string some across the room as mobiles. The first kind is simply and quickly made.

1 Cut two triangles, the same size, out of card. Make a cut half way along the base of both. Now slot them into each other. Spray with gold or silver to get a better effect.

1 Using compasses, draw two circles on a piece of card, using the same centre. The inner circle should be half the diameter of the outer one — e.g. outer 10cms, inner 5cms.

2 Now mark the outside of the circle with a pencil dot every 60 degrees. Half turn the card and mark the inner circle in the same way, but so that the dots alternate with those on the outer circle.

3 Now join up the dots from outer to inner circle and cut out the star shape that is formed. Spray or colour.

Both kinds of star can be hung by thread glued to one tip.

THE WISE MEN

Jesus' own people, the Jews, had waited a long time for the great King that God had promised would one day be born. People in other lands had caught a hint of the news about a coming king of the Jews, so when the wise men saw a special bright star in the eastern sky they were sure that the king had been born. They would find him and bring him their worship and homage. Matthew's Gospel, chapter 2, tells the story.

'Jesus was born in the town of Bethlehem in Judaea, during the time when Herod was king. Soon afterwards, some men who studied the stars came from the east to Jerusalem and asked, "Where is the baby born to be the king of the Jews? We saw his star when it came up in the east, and we have come to worship him."

When King Herod heard about this, he was very upset, and so was everyone else in Jerusalem. He called together all the chief priests and the teachers of the Law and asked them, "Where will the Messiah be born?"

"In the town of Bethlehem in Judaea," they answered. "For this is what the prophet wrote:

'Bethlehem in the land of Judah, you are by no means the least of the leading cities of Judah; for from you will come a leader who will guide my people Israel.' "

So Herod called the visitors from the east to a secret meeting and found out from them the exact time the star had appeared. Then he sent them to Bethlehem with these instructions: "Go and make a careful search for the child and when you find him, let me know, so that I too may go and worship him."

And so they left, and on their way they saw the same star they had seen in the east.

When they saw it, how happy they were, what joy was theirs! It went ahead of them until it stopped over the place where the child was. They went into the house, and when they saw the child with his mother Mary, they knelt down and worshipped him. They brought out their gifts of gold, frankincense, and myrrh, and presented them to him.

Then they returned to their country by another road, since God had warned them in a dream not to go back to Herod.'

Magi were learned men who studied the stars and were also wise in science, mathematics and philosophy. They were good men, studying and seeking truth. No one knows how many made that long journey, nor how they travelled, but we usually imagine three, because there were three gifts. Tradition has added that they were kings.

Legends are told about them and they have been given names. This is how they are usually named and described.

Melchior
Old, with gray hair and beard
King of Arabia and Nubia
His gift was *gold*

Caspar
Young and beardless
King of Sheba
His gift was *frankincense*

Balthazar
Dark-skinned, black beard
King of Tarse and Egypt
His gift was *myrrh*

THE GIFTS

The magi brought splendid gifts to the baby Jesus — gold, frankincense and myrrh.

Frankincense is a sweet-smelling incense used in temple worship and myrrh is a kind of fragrant spice that was used in the preparing of dead bodies for burial. From ancient times Christians have seen special meaning in these three presents.

Gold — king of all metals — was a fit gift for Jesus, King of kings.

Frankincense offered reminds us that Jesus is God, to be worshipped and adored.

Myrrh hints from the very beginning at the coming death of Jesus. He was going to give up his life in order to be the Savior of the world.

King — God — Savior — the wise men said it all.

The wise may bring their learning,
The rich may bring their wealth,
And some may bring their greatness,
And some their strength and health:
We too would bring our treasures
To offer to the King;
We have no wealth or learning,
What gifts then shall we bring?

We'll bring him hearts that love him,
We'll bring him thankful praise,
And souls for ever striving
To follow in his ways:
And these shall be the treasures
To offer to the King,
And these are gifts that ever
Our grateful hearts may bring.

Taken from A TYROLESE CAROL

ESCAPE FROM THE CRUEL KING

Not everyone was happy and glad when Jesus was born. One man was very angry and upset. Herod was king, under the Romans, of the land where Jesus lived. He was a clever king and he had kept law and order in the land. But he was suspicious and jealous of anyone who might try to take his throne away from him. He was cruel and without pity too. Whenever he saw people whispering or talking together, he suspected them of plotting his death. He did not wait to find out if they were innocent. He gave orders for them to be put to death, even when they were members of his own family.

So, although Herod pretended to be pleased and interested in what the wise men had to tell him, he was really furiously jealous. He knew that the baby had been born in Bethlehem. The only safe plan was to kill every baby in that city and so make sure that no new king could survive. His cruelty brought terror and grief to many happy homes. But Jesus was kept safe.

Innocent's Song

Who's that knocking on the window,
Who's that standing at the door,
What are all those presents
Lying on the kitchen floor?

Who is the smiling stranger
With hair as white as gin,
What is he doing with the children
And who could have let him in?

Why has he rubies on his fingers,
A cold, cold crown on his head,
Why, when he caws his carol,
Does the salty snow run red?

Why does he ferry my fireside
As a spider on a thread,
His fingers made of fuses
And his tongue of gingerbread?

Why does the world before him
Melt in a million suns,
Why do his yellow, yearning eyes
Burn like saffron buns?

Watch where he comes walking
Out of the Christmas flame,
Dancing, double-talking:
Herod is his name.

CHARLES CAUSLEY

The Legend
of the Spider's Web

by William Barclay

When Joseph and Mary and Jesus were on their way to Egypt, the story runs, as the evening came they were weary, and they sought refuge in a cave. It was very cold, so cold that the ground was white with hoar frost.

A little spider saw the little baby Jesus, and he wished so much that he could do something for him to keep him warm in the cold night. He decided to do the only thing he could do, to spin his web across the entrance of the cave, to make, as it were, a curtain there.

Along the path there came a detachment of Herod's soldiers, seeking for children to kill to carry out Herod's bloodthirsty order. When they came to the cave, they were about to burst in to search it, to see if anyone was hiding there, but their captain noticed the spider's web. It was covered with the white hoar frost and stretched right across the entrance to the cave.

'Look,' he said, 'at the spider's web there. It is quite unbroken and there cannot possibly be anyone in the cave, for anyone entering the cave would certainly have torn the web.'

So the soldiers passed on, and left the holy family in peace because a little spider had spun his web across the entrance to the cave.

And that, so they say, is why to this day we put tinsel on our Christmas trees, for the glittering tinsel streamers stand for the spider's web, white with the hoar frost, stretched across the cave on the way to Egypt.

It is a lovely story, and this much, at least, is true, that no gift which Jesus receives is ever forgotten.

HOLIDAY TIME

the long summer holidays. Children break up from school in mid-December and are off until the beginning of February. Picnics, swimming, boating, camping and every kind of outdoor activity are part of the whole excitement and enjoyment of Christmas.

In days gone by all holidays were holy days. Christmas was such a special holy day that it was followed by twelve whole days of feasting, free from ordinary work. Just as Advent tells us about God's coming to us, so, the church explained, the Twelve Days of Christmas remind us of our need to come to him.

In the days when most people worked on the land, winter was a good time to take a holiday. Once industry became important, holiday time was cut down from twelve days to two. Expensive machinery could not be left idle for long. In many countries today the trend is towards a break from work lasting from Christmas until after New Year.

In Australia and New Zealand Christmas comes in

GAMES TO PLAY

Even in countries where Christmas comes in winter, sport is important. Football matches and race meetings are often organized for the day after Christmas. Families, too, like to go out for a brisk walk or try out new cycles. If it's freezing or snowing there are lots of other outdoor sports to enjoy. But indoor games have always been popular over Christmas too.

SAYING THANK YOU

As well as giving presents to others, you will have had presents sent to you from friends and others in the family. Remembering to say thank you is important. Why not write 'thank you' letters and cards right away, before you are too busy or forget how pleased you

were with the gifts. Letter-writing can be dull, but you can make it more fun to do — and nicer for those who get your letters — by decorating the paper or cards you write on. Here are two suggestions — you will think of others yourself.

Letters
Make a heading to the paper with patterns or pictures in crayon or felt-tip pens. You could color a border the whole way round, using a chain of little flowers or a zig-zag geometric pattern.

Cards
Use a plain piece of card or fold one in half. Decorate front or outside by glueing on pictures or shapes cut out from some of the prettiest wrapping-paper you received.

THE SPINNER GAME

Here is a game to play that you can make yourselves. It is popular with people of all ages. Grown-ups can stay sitting where they are and there are no pencils, paper or cards to worry with.

To make
First make a list of all kinds of topics. It could include: boy's name; girl's name; name of country; river; town; color; bird; animal; flower; sport; author; artist; musician; politician and so on. You could include: something found in the baker's shop; something to do with Christmas; a book of the Bible and many more that you will think up. Now write each one out neatly on separate small pieces of card. You may need a grown-up's help to make the spinner.

What you need:
1 wooden clothespin
1 nail (1 ½-2 inches long)
1 piece of plywood, 4 ¾ inches square
1 small washer (you can make one out of stiff cardboard)
1 sheet of white paper or cardboard
1 cork

1
Find the centerpoint of the plywood by drawing the diagonals.

2
Bang a nail *squarely* right through at the centerpoint.

3
Draw a circle of not more than 4 ¾ inches diameter on the white card. Divide it into 24 equal sectors, each with a letter of the alphabet in (miss out X and Z).

4
Cut out the circle, push the nail point through the center, and glue it to the wood base with the letters showing.

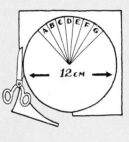

5
Put the washer over the nail.

6
Drill a hole (a little bigger than the nail) through the clothespin, at the center of balance. Sharpen the open ends to a point.

7
Put nail through hole in pin, and make sure it spins freely.

8
Cover sharp tip of nail with a small cork.

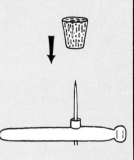

To play
Choose one person to be the caller and judge. He takes a card from the box where you have put them and at the same time twists the spinner. He calls out the subject on the card and the letter it must begin with (for example, a precious stone beginning with E). The first player to call out an answer takes the card. At the end the winner is the one with the most cards.

Papa Panov's Special Christmas

by Leo Tolstoy

It was Christmas Eve and although it was still afternoon, lights had begun to appear in the shops and houses of the little Russian village, for the short winter day was nearly over. Excited children scurried indoors and now only muffled sounds of chatter and laughter escaped from closed shutters.

Old Papa Panov, the village shoemaker, stepped outside his shop to take one last look around. The sounds of happiness, the bright lights and the faint but delicious smells of Christmas cooking reminded him of past Christmas times when his wife had been alive and his own children little. Now they had gone. His usually cheerful face, with the little laughter wrinkles behind the round steel spectacles, looked sad now. But he went back indoors with a firm step, put up the shutters and set a pot of coffee to heat on the charcoal stove. Then, with a sigh, he settled in his big armchair.

Papa Panov did not often read, but tonight he pulled down the big old family Bible and, slowly tracing the lines with one forefinger, he read again the Christmas story. He read how Mary and Joseph, tired by their journey to Bethlehem, found no room for them at the inn, so that Mary's little baby was born in the cow-shed.

'Oh dear, oh dear!' exclaimed Papa Panov, 'if only they had come here! I would have given them my bed and I could have covered the baby with my patchwork quilt to keep him warm.'

He read on about the wise men who had come to see the baby Jesus, bringing him splendid gifts. Papa Panov's face fell.

'I have no gift that I could give him,' he thought sadly.

Then his face brightened. He put down the Bible, got up and stretched his long arms to the shelf high up in his little room. He took down a small, dusty box and opened it. Inside was a perfect pair of tiny leather shoes. Papa Panov smiled with satisfaction. Yes, they were as good as he had remembered — the best shoes he had ever made.

'I should give him those,' he decided, as he gently put them away and sat down again.

He was feeling tired now, and the further he read the sleepier he became. The print began to dance before his eyes so that he closed them, just for a moment. In no time at all Papa Panov was fast asleep.

And as he slept he dreamed. He dreamed that someone was in his room and he knew at once, as one does in dreams, who the person was. It was Jesus.

'You have been wishing that you could see me, Papa Panov,' he said kindly, 'then look for me tomorrow. It will be Christmas Day and I will visit you. But look carefully, for I shall not tell you who I am.'

When at last Papa Panov awoke, the bells were ringing out and a thin light was filtering through the shutters.

'Bless my soul!' said Papa Panov. 'It's Christmas Day!'

He stood up and stretched himself for he was rather stiff. Then his face filled with happiness as he remembered his dream. This would be a very special Christmas after all, for Jesus was coming to visit him. How would he look? Would he be a little baby, as at that first Christmas? Would he be a grown man, a carpenter — or the great King that he is, God's Son? He must watch carefully the whole day

through so that he recognized him however he came.

Papa Panov put on a special pot of coffee for his Christmas breakfast, took down the shutters and looked out of the window. The street was deserted, no one was stirring yet. No one except the road sweeper. He looked as miserable and dirty as ever, and well he might! Whoever wanted to work on Christmas Day — and in the raw cold and bitter freezing mist of such a morning?

Papa Panov opened the shop door, letting in a thin stream of cold air. 'Come in!' he shouted across the street cheerily. 'Come and have some hot coffee to keep out the cold!'

The sweeper looked up, scarcely able to believe his ears. He was only too glad to put down his broom and come into the warm room. His old clothes steamed gently in the heat of the stove and he clasped both red hands round the comforting warm mug as he drank.

Papa Panov watched him with satisfaction, but every now and then his eyes strayed to the window. It would never do to miss his special visitor.

'Expecting someone?' the sweeper asked at last. So Papa Panov told him about his dream. 'Well, I hope he comes,' the sweeper said, 'you've given me a bit of Christmas cheer I never expected to have. I'd say you deserve to have your dream come true.' And he actually smiled.

When he had gone, Papa Panov put on cabbage soup for his dinner, then went to the door again, scanning the street. He saw no one. But he was mistaken. Someone *was* coming.

The girl walked so slowly and quietly, hugging the walls of shops and houses, that it

was a while before he noticed her. She looked
very tired and she was carrying something. As
she drew nearer he could see that it was a baby,
wrapped in a thin shawl. There was such
sadness in her face and in the pinched little face
of the baby, that Papa Panov's heart went out to
them.

'Won't you come in?' he called, stepping
outside to meet them. 'You both need a warm
by the fire and a rest.'

The young mother let him shepherd her
indoors and to the comfort of the armchair. She
gave a big sigh of relief.

'I'll warm some milk for the baby,' Papa
Panov said, 'I've had children of my own — I

can feed her for you.' He took the milk from the
stove and carefully fed the baby from a spoon,
warming her tiny feet by the stove at the same
time.

'She needs shoes,' the cobbler said.

But the girl replied, 'I can't afford shoes, I've
got no husband to bring home money. I'm on
my way to the next village to get work.'

A sudden thought flashed into Papa Panov's
mind. He remembered the little shoes he had
looked at last night. But he had been keeping
those for Jesus. He looked again at the cold little
feet and made up his mind.

'Try these on her,' he said, handing the
baby and the shoes to the mother. The

beautiful little shoes were a perfect fit. The girl smiled happily and the baby gurgled with pleasure.

'You have been so kind to us,' the girl said, when she got up with her baby to go. 'May all your Christmas wishes come true!'

But Papa Panov was beginning to wonder if his very special Christmas wish *would* come true. Perhaps he had missed his visitor? He looked anxiously up and down the street. There were plenty of people about but they were all faces that he recognized. There were neighbors going to call on their families. They nodded and smiled and wished him Happy Christmas! Or beggars — and Papa Panov hurried indoors to fetch them hot soup and a generous hunk of bread, hurrying out again in case he missed the Important Stranger.

All too soon the winter dusk fell. When Papa Panov next went to the door and strained his eyes he could no longer make out the passers-by. Most were home and indoors by now anyway. He walked slowly back into his room at last, put up the shutters and sat down wearily in his armchair.

So it had been just a dream after all.
Jesus had not come.

Then all at once he knew that he was no longer alone in the room.

This was no dream for he was wide awake. At first he seemed to see before his eyes the long stream of people who had come to him that day. He saw again the old road sweeper, the young mother and her baby and the beggars he had fed. As they passed, each whispered, 'Didn't you see *me,* Papa Panov?'

'Who are you?' he called out, bewildered.

Then another voice answered him. It was the voice from his dream — the voice of Jesus.

'I was hungry and you fed me,' he said. 'I was naked and you clothed me. I was cold and you warmed me. I came to you today in every one of those you helped and welcomed.'

Then all was quiet and still. Only the sound of the big clock ticking. A great peace and happiness seemed to fill the room, overflowing Papa Panov's heart until he wanted to burst out singing and laughing and dancing with joy.

'So he *did* come after all!' was all that he said.

'THE QUIET IN THE LAND'

Christmas is a time for children, for noise, excitement and jollity. But Jesus' coming is for all people of all ages. When Mary and Joseph brought him to the Temple for the special service to dedicate a new baby to God, he was welcomed and nursed by two very old people.

Many of the Jews were eagerly awaiting a mighty and magnificent king, who would lead the people to glorious victory against their enemies. But there were others looking for a just and godly Messiah. They were known as 'the Quiet in the Land,' for they spent their days in prayer and worship of God, waiting patiently for the day when he would send his chosen Saviour to earth.

Simeon and Anna were two of the Quiet in the Land. They had waited many years to see God's promised Messiah. As soon as they saw the baby Jesus they recognized him as God's Deliverer, and knew that their dreams were fulfilled. Luke's Gospel tells the story:

'The time came for Joseph and Mary to perform the ceremony of purification, as the Law of Moses commanded. So they took the child to Jerusalem to present him to the Lord, as it is written in the law of the Lord: "Every first-born male is to be dedicated to the Lord." They also went to offer a sacrifice of a pair of doves or two young pigeons, as required by the law of the Lord.

At that time there was a man named Simeon living in Jerusalem. He was a good, devout man and was waiting for Israel to be saved. The Holy Spirit was with him and had assured him that he would not die before he had seen the Lord's promised Messiah. Led by the Spirit, Simeon went into the Temple. When the parents brought the child Jesus into the Temple to do for him what the Law required, Simeon took

88

the child in his arms and gave thanks to God:

"Now, Lord, you have kept
    your promise,
and you may let your
    servant go in peace.
With my own eyes I have
    seen your salvation
which you have prepared in
    the presence of all peoples:
A light to reveal your will to
    the Gentiles
and bring glory to your people
    Israel."

The child's father and mother were amazed at the things Simeon said about him. Simeon blessed them and said to Mary his mother, "This child is chosen by God for the destruction and the salvation of many in Israel. He will be a sign from God which many people will speak against and so reveal their secret thoughts. And sorrow, like a sharp sword, will break your own heart."

There was a very old prophetess, a widow named Anna, daughter of Phanuel of the tribe of Asher. She had been married for only seven years and was now eighty-four years old. She never left the Temple; day and night she worshipped God, fasting and praying. That very same hour she arrived and gave thanks to God and spoke about the child to all who were waiting for God to set Jerusalem free.'

SOMETHING QUIET TO DO

Once Christmas is over it's sometimes nice to find some quiet things to do. Now that the Christmas cards have been taken down, you could sort them through and find things to make from some of them.

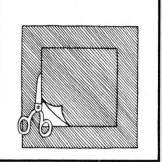

1

Make a picture or calendar from any really special ones, such as reproductions of famous paintings. Find a piece of cardboard larger than the picture and measure out a shape slightly smaller than the picture. Cut that amount of card away and you will be left with a card frame, which you can then glue onto the picture. You can glue a small calendar to the bottom, using two pieces of ribbon.

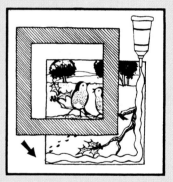

2

Cut out suitable pictures from cards to form gift tags for next year's presents. Make sure you put them away where you can find them at the right time!

3

Cut out scraps for use in collages or ready for use as pictures in next year's Advent calendar.

CHRISTMAS ALL YEAR ROUND

Perhaps most people breathe a sigh when Christmas is over. Grown-ups may breathe a sigh of relief. The upheaval, excitement, expense and hard work that Christmas brings have been quite enough to make them thankful that it is all over for another year. Children may breathe a sigh of disappointment. It seems sad to take down all the decorations, banish the Christmas tree and finish up the last crumbs of Christmas cookies or cake.

But in the church's calendar, Christmas lasts for a whole year. It is March when the church celebrates the coming of the angel Gabriel to tell Mary that she was going to be the mother of the promised Savior, and the following February when Candlemas commemorates the visit of Joseph and Mary to the temple, to dedicate the baby Jesus to God. So a whole year of months is included in the complete Christmas story.

In a more important sense, what began in the manger at Bethlehem lasts the whole year through. Jesus' birth was only the beginning of God's plan to bring light and life to the world. When Jesus chose to become a human being like us, he brought God to us. Although he was a real human baby, he was also God becoming man. He came to tell us all about God and how he feels about us. He came to show, as well as to tell, what God is like.

As he grew up he made God's love known by everything he did. He helped and healed and cared for everyone he met. But from the beginning of time he had a still more wonderful plan for showing us God's love. That love is so great that Jesus willingly died to take away all our wrongdoing and bring us back close to God. Christmas was the beginning that led up to the first Good Friday and Easter Day.

Nothing can ever be the same since that first Christmas. Because of Jesus' birth, his Spirit is with us now and God's love is spread everywhere in the world. For those who invite him, Jesus has come to stay — all the year round.

Love came down at Christmas,
Love all lovely, Love Divine;
Love was born at Christmas,
Star and angels gave the sign.

Worship we the Godhead,
Love Incarnate, Love Divine;
Worship we our Jesus:
But wherewith for sacred sign?

Love shall be our token,
Love be yours and love be mine,
Love to God and all men,
Love for plea and gift and sign.

CHRISTINA ROSSETTI

INDEX

ACKNOWLEDGEMENTS

The author would like to express her special thanks to individuals who have helped with information for particular sections of the book:
Alan Batchelor, pages 33,37,83; Gae Fleming (Australia), pages 42-43; David Lax, page 39; Erica Lineham (New Zealand), pages 28,43; Ron Newby (Church of England Children's Society), pages 34,35; Lynn Prest, page 39.

The material listed below is copyright and is reprinted by kind permission of the copyright holders.

Bible quotations are from *Good News Bible*, copyright 1966, 1971 and 1976 American Bible Society; published by Bible Societies/Collins.

William Barclay, 'The Legend of the Spider's Web', page 81, reprinted by permission of The Saint Andrew Press, from *The Daily Study Bible (Matthew)* by William Barclay.

Dietrich Bonhoeffer, extract from *Letters and Papers from Prison*, pages 66-67, reprinted by permission of SCM Press Ltd.

Carol, *The Kings*, page 73, reprinted by permission from *The Oxford Book of Carols*.

Charles Causley, 'The Innocent's Song', page 80, reprinted by permission of David Higham Associates Limited, from *The Sun, Dancing* by Charles Causley published by Kestrel.

Aileen Fisher, 'A Gift for Gramps', page 57, copyright © 1980 Mala Powers, as it appears in *Follow the Star* published by Hodder and Stoughton and adapted with permission from an original story by Aileen Fisher © 1948.

Eric P. Keely, 'Don Pedro's Christmas', page 54, copyright © 1980 Mala Powers, as it appears in *Follow the Star*, published by Hodder and Stoughton and adapted with permission from the original story by Eric P. Keely © 1939, 1967 by Rand McNally and Company.

David Kossoff, 'Seth' and 'Journey of a Lifetime', pages 51 and 74, reprinted by permission of Collins Publishers from *The Book of Witnesses*.

C.S. Lewis, 'Christmas Comes to Narnia', page 16, from *The Lion, The Witch and the Wardrobe*, copyright C.S. Lewis 1950, published by Collins Publishers. For USA: Reprinted with permission of Macmillan Publishing Company from *The Lion, the Witch and the Wardrobe* by C.S. Lewis, copyright 1950 by C.S. Lewis Pte., Ltd. Copyright renewed.

Eric Marshall and Stuart Hample, *Children's Letters to God*, prayers on pages 10 and 46, reprinted by permission of The Sterling Lord Agency, Inc.; copyright © 1966 by Eric Marshall and Stuart Hample.

Joan Mellings, 'Christmas in Two Lands', page 42, reprinted by permission of the author.

Grace P. Moon, 'Chi-Wee's Special Present', page 22 from *Chi-Wee: The Adventures of a Little Indian Girl* by Grace P. Moon, copyright 1925 by Doubleday and Co. Inc., reprinted by permission of the publisher.

Bernard O'Reilly, 'The Santa Claus of Kanimbla Valley', page 30, reprinted by permission of Mrs R. Kenny from *Green Mountains and Cullenbenbong* by Bernard O'Reilly published by Smith and Paterson Pty Ltd.

Mala Powers, 'Piccola', page 24, copyright © 1980 Mala Powers, as it appears in *Follow the Star*, published by Hodder and Stoughton and adapted with permission from an original story in *My Bookhouse*, edited by Olive Beaupré Miller © 1928.

Hilda Rostron, 'The Shepherds found the Stable', page 48, by Hilda Rostron, from *New Child Songs* © National Christian Education Council and used by permission.

Arthur Scholey, *The Story of Baboushka* reprinted by permission of Lion Publishing. Published as a picture storybook by Lion Publishing; for USA by Crossway Books, Chicago.

Laura Ingalls Wilder, 'Christmas at the Little House in the Big Woods', page 70, reprinted by permission of Methuen Children's Books from *The Little House in the Big Woods*. For USA: reprinted by permission of Harper and Row from *The Little House in the Big Woods* by Laura Ingalls Wilder.